Jesus Inside

A Prison Minister's Memoir and Training Manual

Will Schmit

Published by EA Books Publishing a division of
Living Parables of Central Florida, Inc. a 501c3
EABooksPublishing.com

DEDICATION

Jesus Inside is inspired by, and dedicated to, the living legacy of my Pastor, Donald Wesley. If I am ever half the man he was, I'll be twice the man I am today.

Will Schmit

CONTENTS

ACKNOWLEDGMENTS

My great aunt, Margaret Schmit, 'Markie' to us, was a traveling one room school teacher back in the horse and wagon days. She somehow wound up with a ten foot blackboard in her living room upon which I learned to write, longhand, before ever attending school. She taught me that no matter how many books, letters, or poems I would ever write, the most important words I could ever put to paper are; Thank You.

I want to thank a long list of supporters, and even a few detractors, that have made straight the way of the Lord for our prison ministry. Dale Ormsby, is the first person who comes to mind. Dale never came inside with us but his constant faith in the worthiness of our mission assuaged any personal doubts that threatened to confound our progress.

David Michael grew up just down the road from me in Wisconsin, but we never met until we were in our fifties and discovered our mutual cheese-headedness. David exemplified a willingness to listen as the ordinary opportunities of our lives revealed themselves to be miraculous.

Dan Ely included me in a Saturday morning coffee club that brought church to the sidewalk in the realization that every conversion starts with conversation.

Paul Titus, Michael Buckingham, Richard Brooks and Martin Swett are businessmen that met the financial needs of furthering the ministry. They put their money where my mouth was because it was a brotherly thing to do.

Arthur William Bowen III walked to high school with me every day and forty some years later walked with me in spirit and in truth as I made my way inside the gates of Pelican Bay.

Susan Littman shares a love of reading and considered this a story worth repeating.

The men who joined the ministry: Christian Neaf, Evan Scott, Sid Boney, Matt Niclai, Al Maurer, Michael Hoffman, Roosevelt Whittington III, Cameron English, Dan Weber have put time, heart, and muscle into the equation, "Where two or more are gathered together in My Name I am there also."

Mike Libolt often filled the gas tank of our caravan but how he filled our hearts with encouragement is the real measure of his support.

My editor Alycia Morales helped me convey, in English, what might've remained a 'best intention'.

Only the Lord knows who our anonymous supporters are but I pray we're introduced at the great Resurrection feast!

My wife, Trey, caught a new song in her heart singing with the choir at San Quentin and has kept the beat alive in our household ever since. My Pastor, Donald Wesley, taught me to always defer to her if anyone ever asked me if I was a follower of Jesus Christ as only her testimony could ever hope, or dare, to recommend me. Thank you, Trey, for being the reason any of my words ring true.

FOREWORD

It is interesting to me that when Jesus spoke about what people did and did not do, it wasn't about Scripture memorization, church attendance, or paying your tithes. It was all summed up into, "Did you care about the hungry? Whom did you feed? How did you treat those dying of thirst? Where there was nakedness, did you provide clothing? Did you welcome the strangers and visit to the sick? How about prison...did you go to the prisons?"

Not many of us have ever walked into a prison, looked in the eyes of a criminal and said, "By the way no matter what, Jesus loves you. "Will Schmit does just that and has made it his life's mission to shake hands with inmates and offer them the unconfined hope of Jesus Christ.

This Prison Minister's Memoir and Training Manual provides all the tools you'll need to connect with the lowest in serving the Most High. Reading Jesus Inside will give you the how to, as well as the why, the who, the what, and the when and where. This book will challenge you to reach beyond yourself, beyond the walls of jails and penitentiaries to bring the message of hope, the Gospel of Jesus Christ.

The other thing I felt while reading Jesus Inside, was Will's heart for the captive. He has a contagious passion and I hope that you become infected with it, and never recover.

They are waiting...

Rudy Trussler
Eureka, CA
Author of Mud, Blood & Cardboard

FOREWORD

As a child, I could be rescued from poor choices. The store owner who caught me shoplifting simply called my dad and my sentence was a stiff lecture and an in-house imprisonment. As I got older, my poor choices were met with stiffer punishment. My parents could not simply ask the nice police officer to dismiss my speeding ticket.

Fortunately, good decisions…with a lot of grace and help from others…began to move me in a healthy direction. In fact, it was the "help from others" part that led me to pursue a career as a minister. I am well aware that a steady diet of bad choices combined with difficult circumstance could see me in a very different setting…prison.

The Bible teaches us that we followers of Christ all have a "part to play" in this thing called the "body". I could not do what I do were it not for the multitudes of fellow believers all playing their part in doing God's work in this fallen world.

Will Schmit is a friend who plays his part. In his whimsical, yet hard-hitting manner he writes an operational manual that strikes at the heart of the reader. Most "manuals" are prescriptions for insomnia. Jesus Inside captures the critical points of dynamic prison ministry in story form, weaving his own experience with the how to's of working with inmates. His cynicism, wit and humor capture the environment on "the inside".

To say this work is inspiring sounds trite, but it is. You'll be laughing on one page only to be weeping on another. Jesus Inside will draw you into a journey—a journey of real people and living real lives. Far from falling asleep, you'll get a sense that you're reading a well plotted suspense novel and upon completion you'll be encouraged—not only with what is happening in prison ministry, but the part YOU can play in the adventure.

As a long time Pastor in the local church, it is refreshing to read a resource that is practical, engaging, and timely. Pastors, lay workers, prayer warriors, in fact anyone with a sense of compassion will benefit from reading this book. So, what are you waiting for? Turn the page… "start the music…it's time to dance".

Neil Montgomery,
Congregational Care Pastor,
Scottsdale Bible Church,
Scottsdalebible.com

INTRODUCTION

If you are reading this book you might be thinking about Prison Ministry. This ministry is unique and requires a special consecration because the people you are going to minister are criminals who committed serious crimes. They deserve punishment... yet, they are human beings and souls, who also were created by God. Therefore, there is a hope for them too. Despite all odds these people are in God's plan for salvation; there is hope they might become citizens of the Kingdom of Heaven. This is prison ministry.

I was resistant to this ministry myself. Then I became a Chaplain at Pelican Bay State Prison (PBSP) and my perception of this ministry was changed forever. Many inmates are lost souls for Heaven. However, there is hope for them. They need help! Maybe you are the one who will help them? If so, God bless you in this faith journey.

Jesus Inside is about one man's faith journey in prison ministry. Two years ago I met Will Schmit for the first time at PBSP. He brought another fellow minister and... saxophone (!). I thought, what a blessing (saxophone!), since our inmates don't play any instruments (so far).

The population of our prison consists of those who violated the Law in their early years. Most of them are from broken families, who never finished school. They had no time for music. Each inmate's story is a combination of a social problems, physical abuse, drugs and wrong decisions.

One of these wrong decisions was to escape their misery. The "way" to escape was to join a local gang where they found "sense of family", easy money which are bloody money. Now, these inmates were listening Will's instrumental performance... it was a blessing for everybody.

Then Will began to preach... directly to their hearts. That was a real blessing. He used simple words, phrases and stories... but these were so effective and straight to the point. Every month for two years inmates still ask when Will's group will come again.

This book is very useful since it doesn't give lengthy theological justification for prison ministry, but provides simple truth, coined by Jesus Christ – "Love the Lord your God with all your heart and with all your soul and with all your mind and "Love your neighbor as yourself". Who is my neighbor? Well, inmates are our neighbors too! Regardless what they have done, they can be saved by God's Grace.

Jesus Inside provides a great illustration of this truth through various examples of interaction with inmates. This ministry has various aspects – from imparting simple Bible truth to safety and security issues (after all you are in prison!). Many of these aspects are covered in this book in a most efficient way. Therefore, this book will help you to learn a lot about prison ministry.

As a Chaplain I am blessed to have Will Schmit's team at PBSP. I believe that Jesus Inside will inspire more of God's people to become volunteers/ministers at prison. After all, what can be better than to bring lost soul to God?

Rev. Alexander Valuiski,
Chaplain at Pelican Bay State Prison

Chapter One

In the Beginning was the "Who me?"

Ever wonder how God might call you into service? It might be as simple as looking into the mirror and recognizing the need for a haircut. In the summer of 1995 I drove downtown to a new barbershop hoping to sell a water filtration system to the proprietor. As I waited my turn to pull into the parking garage I noticed two men sitting together in the town square. I pulled into a space, got out of the car, adjusted my suit, grabbed my briefcase and felt my legs lock up. I'd had sciatic episodes before, especially when wearing dress shoes, so I braced myself for a shooting pain to jump up from the sidewalk into my hips and lower back. But the pain didn't come.

I glanced back at the two men in the center of town and took a few tentative steps away from my car. Relieved, I aimed again for the hair salon but felt my feet stiffen as if I'd slipped into a pair of cement boots. I sensed the only way I'd make it to my appointment was to go the opposite direction and make a series of left turns. I tried that and it worked. Weird.

This course adjustment brought me within ear shot of the two men I'd noticed earlier and when I neared their location, I slowed to listen and observe. After all, you never know who might need a water filter. The men were speaking quietly, with an attitude of reverence, and one of them held the largest Bible I'd ever seen. I'd been raised Catholic, so I knew enough to let people alone when they were praying.

As I was about to move on, the men said, "Amen." So I approached them and asked if they needed any filtration services. They didn't, but their smiles made me want to stick around. After a little small talk they introduced themselves as members of the House of Refuge Christian Fellowship and invited me to come by some Sunday and check it out. I wasn't really a church go-er, although my wife and I had recently begun attended services to appease her five year old daughter's insistence that we listen to a friend of hers sing in a children's choir.

The Pastor, a certain Donald Wesley I was to learn, mentioned they met at the YMCA every Sunday at 10:30. As it was by now past the time of my hair appointment, I thanked them for the invite and, without a thought to my feet working rapidly no matter which direction I faced, hurried off to get my haircut. It was weeks before I thought about my encounter, but one Sunday when we were free of our watch the neighbor kid in the choir obligation I suggested to my wife that we attend the House of Refuge.

"House of Refuge?" she replied. "I could really use a House of Refuge."

We drove into town and dove into a packed room of charismatic chaos. The crowd was racially mixed between Hispanic, Black and, as we came to be called, Caucasoid families. We weren't sure if we were late but something was already in full swing. Ladies were laying overcoats over other ladies laying on the floor, one lady had raised herself up a few inches by standing on her Bible and a trio of singers were beginning a say and sway chorus at the front of the room.

I remember sitting still, more still than I had been since maybe waiting for the principal in sixth grade. Even the drive home was marked with silence, which was unusual as I can't back out of the driveway without having my driving habits critiqued. I asked my wife what she thought of the service and she asked me the same thing. After taking a breath to steady myself for a possible battle of opinions I said, "I think we're home."

My wife relaxed at my sudden conversion to reasonableness and agreed we had found what we were looking for without knowing what it was that was missing in our lives. We took refuge in spirited worship and solace in Pastor Wesley's personal tutelage. One of his first lessons explained that the problem with Christianity was always the Christians, and never Christ. He stressed and exemplified that we should live in such a way as to be a building block, and not a stumbling stone, to anyone constructing a life of faith.

The foundation of Pastor Wesley's ministry was visiting inmates at San Quentin State Prison and within months of our first meeting he invited my wife and I to come along on a visit. We filled out our paperwork and waited. A popular Christian bumper-sticker says, "God doesn't call the qualified. He qualifies the called." We weren't sure we fit into either category but we had a willing spirit and Pastor was certain God would work with that.

"The best is yet to come," was the answer Pastor gave every time we asked him for an update on our paperwork. The waiting game was a central theme to Pastor's Christianity and he based it on Matthew 25:31 "When the Son of Man comes in His glory, and all the holy angels with Him, then He will sit on the throne of His glory. All the nations will be gathered before Him, and He will separate them one from another, as a shepherd divides his sheep from the goats.

And He will set the sheep on His right hand, but the goats on the left. Then the King will say to those on His right hand, 'Come, you blessed of my Father, inherit the kingdom prepared for you from the foundation of the world: For I was hungry and you gave Me food; I was thirsty and you gave Me something to drink; I was a stranger and you took Me in, I was naked and you clothed Me; I was in prison and you came to Me.'"

The idea that he might miss an opportunity to serve "the least of these My brethren," terrified him to the point that rather than finance a church building and incur operating costs he kept the storehouse of the House of Refuge ready to provide food, shelter, or whatever emergency help the congregation might need.

After a few weeks our clearance went through and we found ourselves in the church van parked outside the gates of San Quentin. The wide blue San Francisco Bay and the bright lights of the city reflecting on the water made a spectacular backdrop to the concrete and barbed wire peninsula that is home to approximately 4,000 inmates. San Quentin first opened, and closed, its gates in 1852. It is the longest continually operating prison in the California state system and houses the only death row for male inmates in the state.

We weren't there to sight see but it was hard to pass under the surrounding guard towers without gawking at the sniper guards behind the glass turrets. The first checkpoint, a guard at a window checking photo I.D.s against the approved to visit list, gives way to an anteroom with sliding cage doors at either end, and another armed guard. A final steel door opens to a central courtyard with a green lawn, keep off the grass signs, and a rose garden. Lavender tinged Sterling roses grew waist high along the path to the chapel and, like confused bees, we gathered around the flowers unsure if protocol would allow us to stop and smell the roses.

The chapel, well-lit and spacious, could hold 300 or so in the pews with room for a full 30 person choir on the main stage and a raised side platform for the band. Stained glass and praise banners gave color to the tall walls, chalkboards displayed the dusty echoes of earlier Bible verses and song selections. Bibles, hymnals, and study guides got shuffled as we made our way into the first two rows of the visitor section and waited for the inmates to join us.

Suddenly a sea of sky blue shirts, darker blue pants, and tennis shoes began jostling through the door and our heads turned toward the chatter, each of us being careful not to look like we're looking. The faces are too young, and too old for me to reconcile with being in prison. They are mostly black and Hispanic, some were tattooed in garish gang styles up to the neck, and some look so squeaky clean they could be librarians setting up to debate the logical placement of periodicals.

It was clear the inmates loved Pastor Wesley and, by extension, any visitors he brought with him. A long line of smiling faces waited to shake his hand and say hello and as each man finished with Pastor they came by our pew to welcome us and introduce themselves. The greeting period came to a close as a trio of singers set up microphones and waited for the band to settle in. The first notes of the song had me check my seat to see if I hadn't been transported from San Quentin Chapel to the Apollo Theatre.

The vocal harmonies were intricate, sonorous, and passionate. The band was tight, precise and powerful. The music took direction from an enthusiastic inmate, Kevin Kemp, who seemed intent on drawing angels down from heaven to lift the roof off the chapel. The raucous call and response of the congregation led Pastor Wesley to improvise praise lyrics on the spot. I had never seen, or heard, worship music like that and kept glancing at the ceiling certain that God would part the roof with His smile.

After the music calmed down Pastor waved me up to the podium and handed me his big Bible. "Read 2nd Chronicles," he said, "Chapter Seven, verses fourteen to fifteen."

I didn't do a head count but I knew every eye in the place was on me, the stranger, as I settled behind the podium. The verse he asked me to read was short. Simple. I may have even read it before on a coffee mug or a desk calendar, but I knew I had never read it out loud.

As I fidgeted with the microphone to create an impression that I had done this a thousand times before Pastor leaned into me and whispered, "Until a real Apostle shows up, you're it. No tags back." It was instantly plain and permissible to admit I was in over my head, but isn't that the direction we always aim our prayers? The verse was 2 Chronicles 7:14-15, "If my people who are called by My name will humble themselves, and pray and seek My face, and turn from their wicked ways, then I will hear from heaven, and will forgive their sin and heal their land. Now My eyes will be open and My ears attentive to prayers made in this place."

The Amen that came from the crowd was particular to Black church culture but it was also specifically unique to prison chapel where the underlying theme of any tumult is to tear the roof off the building. Pastor thanked me, called me Doctor Will and had me take a high backed seat at the side of the altar as if I represented every Pope and hope that followed the sign of the cross.

My outside friends question why in the world would I want to volunteer my time to bring the Gospel inside a prison. Truth be known my outside friends didn't see much value in bringing the Gospel anywhere, but the notion of cozying up to convicts and killers seemed an awful waste of a perfectly good week end. I thought of that as I watched Pastor preach to the wave of holy hands in the air and the rush of young men to the kneeling pad at the foot of the altar when Pastor offered a time of private prayer. My most sincere prayer up until that time had been grace before meals, some meals more than others, so when he directed me to kneel down and respond to the inmates prayer requests I uttered the second most sincere prayer in my life. God help me.

Prison etiquette dictates you never ask an inmate about his crime. Confessions do happen, maybe more frequently than in an ordinary church, but they mustn't be solicited. God already knows who's who and what's what. What I'm curious to know about how men the same age as my children earned life sentences is not for me to know and definitely not part of forming common prayer.

Pastor later told me when you're face to face with broken people to remember Jesus was there first and the important thing to do is simply make eye contact and listen. Any tendency to impress with eloquent prayer style and spiritualized word choice is held hostage against an inmate's ability to discern what's really going down. No one cares what you know until they know you care. Soul safety is the only legitimate goal of taking on a brother's burden.

Prayer is a customary and cultural thing. Scripture (Romans 8:26) tells us flat out we don't know what to pray for, the important thing is knowing to Whom we pray. The first young man's back that I touched was bent to the ground and broad enough to support all I knew about being in another man's shoes.

We said the 'Our Father' together as I didn't know any better, not that there's a better prayer to know. We made a claim under the vaulted ceiling of an old cafeteria turned chapel to be family, sons of the same heavenly

Sire. Pastor explained the handshakes we exchanged when we got back to our feet, in that heavily guarded temple, were brotherly clasps of eternal consequence. If the young man and I never met again in this life we'd still be capable of recognition, maybe even seat saving, at Christ's banquet with His bride.

"We'll all get new white robes at the feast," he said. "You've already got the T-shirt, get ready for the rest."

A few dozen men came to the front for prayer that evening, some were likely repeaters, some imitators, some stood in sort of a second row to lend support, and one or two seemed to just be stretching their legs for something to do, but the movement forward meant something. Steps had been taken, maybe ordained by the Lord, and the shuffle back to the seats looked like the last play of a football game. Whatever burden the men brought into the room, they left it on the field and were ready to receive whatever Pastor's sermon was going to bring them.

I've heard hundreds of Pastor's talks, and while I can hardly remember a single word, I can still feel every note he struck in our hearts. The inmates shouted and reached for the stars to match his high points and groaned in accompaniment to his quieter conclusions, but there was never any showmanship, no pounding the podium for emphasis, no cape coming out of the backroom. If Pastor wanted a response he'd simply say, "Oh, you're not listening," and close his Bible, for about a second.

The earnestness he poured into 'the guys' was his main message. They called him to be the father they never had until they got to know the Father that sent His Son to find them, the lost. Lifers, first years, shy folks, and happy grinners counted themselves as sheep in his flock, and because they'd all been black sheep somewhere else, regardless of race, they appreciated being found again and again.

Most of the time I sat with the ladies from the church in the front two rows and watched Pastor's wife, Gabrielle, and daughters eat up the affection the men showered on them from a safely supervised arm's length. If I was part of the program I might stay up on the platform and watch the service unfold like a miniature version of the Red Sea parting. I didn't have a lot of Black Church Cultural experience but I often sensed a boatload of angels just waiting in the wings for a sign to take us home.

Going home meant filing out past the guards, shuffling through the gates, and the hour long ride back to the church parking lot; but the highlight of the return trip was Pastor's main recruiting tool—a stop at a full blown

Jewish delicatessen for huge bowls of Matzo Ball soup and chocolate éclairs that weighed upwards of a pound. We'd fill up a table the length of the backroom and find out more about our fellow ministers of reconciliation than we ever cared, or hoped to know.

Table talk allowed Pastor some time to decompress, a time to joke and tease and build up the body of believers by giggling and being silly. Eager to find my way in the belly laughing bosom of the Lord I once, to my shame, convinced Gabrielle that the word 'gullible' had been removed from the dictionary, because nobody used it anymore. It was even funnier watching her try to convince her sisters of this startling development.

Besides organizing our visits and preaching for an hour or more, Pastor also drove the church van. Under the guise of keeping him awake, riding shotgun afforded opportunity for instruction and insight into what building Christian fellowship with inmates entailed. "Never make promises, never give money, never give your home address, never doubt the inmate's guilt, or repentance. There but for the grace of God go a lot of people that should know better," was Pastor's way of saying Christians shrunk their faith if they degraded jailhouse confessions.

Pastor dedicated his life to being a positive influence on the yard, especially when he wasn't there. Bringing light to a world of darkness doesn't translate to flashes of brilliance as much as setting candles on a birthday cake. Even in a room of strangers, like a bar or a family restaurant, when somebody brings in a birthday cake all heads turn toward the spectacle and whether we know the name of the birthday celebrant or not, we're very likely to join in the singing. That's how Pastor spread the Gospel inside San Quentin.

Being born again meant we became slices of Jesus' birthday cake and Jesus became the never go out candle shining through our lives. Pastor felt it was our mission to spark and kindle little candelabras among the inmates. Get two or more fellows to shine together and create more light for their community than expecting single saints to carry the load of being good examples.

Scripture counsels that two or more joined together gives way to the presence of the Lord in their midst. To make such joining more likely Pastor encouraged men to take time to study Scripture with one, or two, other brothers. This was problematic for a number of reasons, reading ability being chief and foremost. The fear of embarrassing himself with poor vocal presentation has kept many a man silent in the free world, behind bars the impact is magnified.

"The Word of God is living and active, and sharper than any two edged sword, piercing even to the division of soul and spirit, of joints and marrow, and is a discerner of the thoughts and intents of the heart (Hebrews 4:12)." Pastor made a point of encouraging men to practice putting the Word of God on their tongues in small doses to feel the gentleness Spirit holds for the earnest believer. If the only Scripture a man could recite comfortably was, "Jesus wept (John 11:35)" then Pastor wanted the man to know that even that little bit fed the souls of all who heard him read it.

It is important to encourage intimidated readers to trust God to move them along the path to being intrepid exhorters without finishing difficult words or passages for them, as any perceived impatience in the listener will trip up the fledgling orator. "Sound it out, search it out, send it out." Pastor said, "Remember what the Scripture says, "So shall my word be that goes forth from my mouth, it shall not return to me void, but it shall accomplish what I please, and it shall prosper in the thing for which I sent it."" Isaiah 55:11

The miracle of a grown man reading aloud for the first time in his adult life was often repeated at San Quentin, and when I finally began a prison ministry of my own, it became a stalwart operating principle. Courage is the first sign of a deep change taking place. As a man stands, and waits for the room to quiet down for him to read, the temptation to sit, or show off, must be brushed aside. Holding a book open in public opens a man to ridicule, criticism, and a barrage of memories of failing as a student or child.

A simple technique to reinforce the positive effect of successfully reading out loud is to thank the reader and ask him how he feels about reading the verse again, in case anyone in the room wasn't listening. The simple request to repeat a passage gives the reader a chance to absorb what just happened and apply himself to the task with a shade more confidence.

We're told we all love the sound of our own voice, but that's not always the case. If you have a stuttering, stammering presentation the loudest sound you hear when you read is the swell of laughter you imagine building throughout the audience. We often talked about reading Scripture as a healing for both the reader and the listener. The Bible is not just a story book. It has been read under duress and persecution for countless generations and the history of those readings can sometimes be sensed in a man's effort to stop shaking long enough to get the words out of his mouth and into a person's heart.

An inmate from Jamaica, serving a life sentence, told me that reading the words of Jesus, the red letters in his Bible, told him what kind of day it was the same way other people used a calendar to determine the days of the week. He often took to heart Jesus' final words to the thief hanging on the cross, "Assuredly I say to you, today you will be with Me in Paradise (Luke 23:43)." He had an insight that he didn't have to pass from this world to make that statement true and it became a lamp onto his feet as he walked out his time in the yard.

Chapter Two

Find a Need and Spill It

The next time I stepped into a prison yard was four years and three thousand miles later. My family and I had moved to North Carolina, the eastern buckle of the Bible Belt. Our search for a church led us through great and small halls of worship. One neighborhood church might raise thirty or forty souls a Sunday for three hour services and across the street, a mega church would need police help to park all the cars going in and out of three scheduled services housing over a thousand people.

Believers were the rule, not the exception, and most carried rules about what a believer ought to believe. Being a non-denominational proletarian I was often seen as paddling on a different tributary of the River of Life, but I liked the fellowship I found in the faith community and learned to play my part as the brother from a different planet. What I had in common with the more active members of any church we joined or visited was a passion, a spirit for service.

The church we eventually called home used a Sunday every year to postpone services in order to be of service to the community at large. Volunteer groups with the Life Community Church in Wilmington, North Carolina logo T-shirts would meet early in the morning to paint schools, pick up trash, fix up porches and cabinets for shut-ins, or do light landscaping. I somehow got the idea to put together such a volunteer crew to do similar handy man work for the New Hanover County Detention Center. I made some phone calls to the local facility, scheduled a clearance interview and recruited a few able bodies to paint the prison chapel and repair some windows.

While waiting in the director's office for our guest work crew applications I noticed a large annual calendar on the wall with a series of red circles making the six p.m. slot throughout the entire year. Ever curious, especially when beleaguered with country music from the radio, I asked the director what the red circles might mean. "Oh those," he said without looking up from his one fingered typing project. "That's a spot always open in the chapel. Can't ever get anyone to come up and preach at that time as that's when the men are busy getting their laundry, medications, and supper."

"How long's it been that way?" I asked him. "Long as I been here, and that's going on eighteen years," he said.

The first Sunday in question was Hallowe'en, so me dressing up like a preacher seemed appropriate. He penciled in my name, asked the name of my church and how long I'd been ordained. California security and ordination would look good on the application but I needed local credentials and references. I took the form home sensing the blanks on the wall would fill in. All I had to do was convince my church they now had a prison ministry and they needed to ordain me to head it up.

The work crew got more paint on the doors than on our pants but the true measure of our success had more to do with a change in our hearts. One of our volunteers had a relative inside, his father. They hadn't seen each other in three years and weren't really allowed to visit under the circumstance, but one of the guards made sure the painting table was in earshot of the inmates activity yard.

We cleaned the gutters, replaced window screen, and threw in some impromptu tree trimming as my son, Robert, contributed his personal skill set. At the end of the day we probably looked like a gang of pirates just back from burying treasure, but the treasure we uncovered that afternoon neither rusts nor worries about thieves breaking in to steal. The thieves were already there, giving us applause as we packed our tools and made our way back through the gate.

I made an appointment with our church's lead Pastor, Tim Blevins, and filled out my application. I was a little nervous because the last church I encouraged to start up a prison ministry said, "They already tried that, but the state wanted them to ordain someone and they just didn't have the resources for that.' At the time I thought that was some kind of answer. I didn't know it was a question begging to be asked.

Tim heard me out, laughed at the right places and asked me what I thought about the opportunity. "Two or more gathered together in my Name is the minimum He's asking for," I said. "Anything on top of that is gravy." I mentioned I had, in a way, been trained by following my home Pastor to San Quentin for all those years and I would of course consult with him and keep everybody appraised of what was developing, there was just the small detail of getting ordained in North Carolina.

He came around the table smiling and dropped a hand on my shoulder and said, "I think we can handle that. It seems like God's putting you in place for something, so let's consider you ordained." He went on to explain his wife had been praying for two years for someone to come along and lead a prison ministry and he knew God answers prayers. Once again I found myself being part of someone else's prayer.

I turned in my application with a letter of reference on church letterhead and waited to see what part Trick or Treat would play in my attempt to present the Gospel of Jesus Christ. I got to the prison early, way early. I double checked the Scriptures I outlined on a few 3X5 cards and, dressed in my best shirt and tie, I strode up to the gate where I was informed there was no service scheduled. Trick.

I told the guard it wasn't a regularly scheduled service, it was more of an experiment to see if anyone would be interested in such a thing. The guard called a duty sergeant who somehow found my name in the system and agreed to escort me to the chapel and announce my presence over the loudspeaker, not that he thought it would do much good. I sat in the back of the chapel for half an hour smelling the fumes from the freshly painted doors. Alone. I turned to look over my shoulder at a blackened window because I thought I heard the Holy Ghost whisper, "Now you know how I feel."

Two inmates strolled in the building laughing and joking and went stone silent when they saw me come up from the last pew. "Sorry sir, we didn't know anybody was in here. Do you want us to wait outside?"

"No, no, not at all." I stuck my hand out to shake theirs to stop mine from shaking. "You're just in time for the six o' clock service. Come on in."

"There ain't no six o' clock service."

"There is now," I said. Two or more gathered together in my Name means I AM there also, so here we are, either of you sing?"

Our first service stretched on for almost fifteen minutes before the regulars started drifting in for the normal seven o' clock service. I shook as many hands as I could reach at both doors and invited everybody to come out a little earlier next week for the new six o' clock service. A few folks pointed out there wasn't any six o' clock service and my two stalwarts piped up to say, "There is now. Two or more gathered together is all it takes to make a church up in here."

I wasn't sure what my feet were up to as I walked back to my car. It seemed I was walking taller despite stepping into some mighty big boots. The service was unorthodox to put it mildly. We never did make an altar call, or call for testimonies, or prayer requests.

All we did was get excited about being together and search Scripture for our next move. My best shirt was drenched. Baptism by perspiration.

As I drove under the spreading oaks on my way home, the moon flickered in between the branches above me. The sporadic light reminded me of a ceiling lamp struggling to bring light to a long abandoned room, from there it was easy for me to imagine Jesus barking out orders to set another table for the wedding feast. NCDOC 1510 would be attending and it felt great to know I'd have a place to sit with some new friends.

The next Sunday was an important milestone. I'd be able to measure the impact of our new spontaneously ordained ministry and, as it was in the height of football season, and finally turning cold, I'd be able to sport the beautiful leather Green Bay Packer jacket my wife bought me for our anniversary. Knowing that Vince Lombardi gathered the team together for the Our Father before every game, and maybe after, I felt pretty justified bringing my colors to chapel.

I also wore my father's mid-sixties Packer tie, which although it maintained the proper color scheme was a hideous thing that I dragged out occasionally to emphasize my humility. As I crossed the yard to the chapel a few shouts and hollers rang out of the twilight. Shadowed clusters of inmates held their place in the laundry line, or scurried to get to the mess hall before the doors closed, but it seemed I was generating some interest in the community. The guard unlocked the door for me and I strode inside to await the oncoming masses hungry for the word of God.

Forty minutes of less than serene solitude later a few fellows strolled in for the seven o' clock service. Noticing my jacket they good naturedly bemoaned my choice of football loyalties and told me everybody was watching the game and I should've stayed home myself to watch. I surrendered to logic and asked him the score. He gave me a sign with his lower lip indicating he didn't know and scooted out to the common room to find out.

A dozen guys came back with him to see the fool that didn't know team colors were forbidden by the NC Dept. of Corrections and a few more came with them to see what kind of Packer fan gave up Sunday Night Football to come out to preach to an empty room. Our two, or more, grew to nearly two dozen. Enough to field a team. I explained to them that as far as Christianity was concerned, we were the varsity squad.

"When we get to heaven, I said Jesus promises us new white robes. Well here you are gentlemen and you've already got the T-shirts, now it's time to put on the rest of the uniform. Everybody stand up and look at your shoes. Ephesians 6:15 says we "shod our feet with the preparation of the gospel of peace." And Isaiah 52:7 says, "How beautiful upon the mountain are the feet of him who brings good news, Who proclaims peace, Who brings glad tidings of good things, who proclaims salvation, who says to Zion, Your God reigns!"

"Look around you. You are the living epistles in this yard. You might not have faith in your abilities, but I urge you to trust God to be a lamp onto your feet and show you the steps to take to bring light into darkness and make the path secure. And I pray for us all that if anyone is watching us to see what a life of faith and prayer would be, that we would be a building block to the Body of Christ and not a stumbling stone to anybody. Amen."

Our second service assembled and dismissed in about that same time as it would take a two minute warning to set the stage for Green Bay's come from behind victory. "Follow your blockers and run for daylight." Lombardi's sound advice for running backs applies equally to jailhouse preachers.

The week between services took it's normal seven day course but felt like an eternity until I walked back in the yard. Three men were waiting at the door for the chapel to be unlocked. Two or more, gathered together, early, for the service 'nobody would come to.' I shook their hands, re-introduced myself and asked their names hoping I could remember them and build some rapport. "I'm John, " said the first inmate, and the second, and the third. First John, Second John, and Just John, our congregation had its first apostles.

The men hit the lights, showed me how to fill out the volunteer sign in sheet and smiled brighter than a toothpaste commercial. We started to pray for our service and by the time I opened my eyes our number swelled by another two gentleman. Every time a new person walked in I stopped to acknowledge them, introduce myself, ask their name, and tell them to sit close. As long as their name wasn't John they were welcome to stay.

We started a practice of asking for a volunteer to stand and read an opening passage of Scripture. If we had more than one translation in the room, and we almost always did, we'd have each version represented. Some men, being traditionalists preferred the King James, 'the Bible that God used' as it was often referred to in Black Gospel culture, some used the Gideon handed out by the Department of

Corrections, and a few used modern translations.

Because the reading skills varied from man to man, just the act of standing to read was often a courageous act, and sometimes it was a prayer in itself to be useful to the kingdom. Discussion sometimes went to personal reaction to the verse, but this night I asked the question, "Do the actual words of the Word of God matter as much as the meaning?" Is one translation more correct, holier, or more powerful than another, and how did we wind up with so many different versions with a promise of more to come?"

I wasn't after an answer, as much as participation. Church attendance for men, especially inside, is often a spectator sport, or at most a diversion from a schedule where each day is the same as the last and the one to come. If a hand was quick to go in the air it almost made sense to call on the man sitting next to the more willing participant. Invariably the man would protest that he didn't put his hand up, and invariably I'd say I saw something in his eye that prompted me to call on him.

1 Peter 3:15, says, "Be ready, in season and out, to give a defense for the hope that is in you." Every believer is being watched by a cloud of witnesses, some celestial, and some waiting in the shadows with their arms crossed against their chests in defiance, or perhaps, curiosity. The hope is that the Gospel message will ring true from one person's willingness to share it regardless of his eloquence, education, or efficiency.

The point we tried to make is that a man might hear the same message, even the same Scripture, from two different sources and relate better to one than the other for cultural reasons. I used the example of the 12 step programs, 'one drunk helping another' one sinner/saint helping another find something personably relatable in the story of Jesus coming for us, standing in for us in the war against death and the devil. The ultimate responsibility is God's to call onto Him whom He calls as it says in Exodus 33:19, "I will have mercy on whomever I will have mercy, and I will have compassion on whomever I will have compassion.' Our job, our reasonable service, is to make the road to a relationship with Christ smooth and level. That might mean picking up litter in the church yard, or it might mean listening to a hard case complain about injustice or hopelessness.

Our prayer request line that night included the situation of an older man who had attempted suicide a few hours before service after receiving a 'dear Jorge' letter from home. I asked the men to make a point of searching the man out to tell him that I personally was glad he wasn't dead and to tell him that I had once attempted to take my own life and I was looking forward to meeting him next Sunday to compare our stories.

Fifteen minutes before the next service Jorge sat in the center seat in the back row, arms folded, as if daring me to pick him out. I made my usual rounds through the aisles, shaking hands, greeting the new comers, all the time watching him watch me with his one good eye. I stood still when I got to his row and asked an inmate to introduce me. When he gave me his hand I said, "Jorge, if the pills I took, and the razors I set out next to the bathtub when I was twenty two, did what I planned them to do, we'd never have this handshake. I want you to do me a favor. Remember this handshake and see if you can't stick around long enough to tell a stranger a similar story, say ten, or twenty years from now. Can you do that for me?"

Jorge didn't answer, but he didn't let go of my hand either, so I sat down. The man looked ready to cry, but not ready to break the emotional pattern that got him into the mess in the first place. I decided to take a chance to see if I could draw him out into the open and leaned over the chair to whisper in his ear. "Jorge, I know your heart is going to heal because mine did. Jesus promises to bind up the broken hearted, but do you want to know what the real miracle here is?"

"No, Pastor." He whispered. 'Tell me."

"Jorge, the real miracle is that a woman loved us enough to break our hearts in the first place, because you got to admit we're a couple of ugly suckers."

Jorge guffawed all across the back of the chair. We both laughed till our faces hurt and when we finally caught our breath I asked if he would kindly open up the service by reading from Isaiah 61. "The Spirit of the Lord is upon Me, because the Lord has anointed Me to preach good tidings to the poor; He has sent Me to heal the brokenhearted, to proclaim liberty to the captives, and the opening of the prison to those who are bound; …to comfort all who mourn, to console those who mourn in Zion, to give them beauty for ashes, the oil of joy for mourning, a garment of praise for the spirit of heaviness, that they may be called trees of righteousness, the planting of the Lord, that He be glorified."

Jorge became solid as an oak tree and never missed a Sunday service until his sentence was complete and he re-joined his family. His daughter, who had been running the streets on methamphetamines, got sober and came back to live with Jorge and his wife. She credited his letters from jail as being a big reason she turned her life around.

Jorge's last day inside was Christmas Eve, the same day as my last service as a volunteer outreach minister at NHDOC. At the end of the service Jorge came up to the pulpit and said he had something to show me. He pulled out a letter from his wife and daughter welcoming him home, and gave me a handshake that he said he'd be practicing for the next ten, or twenty years.

We figured we'd not see each other again until we met in paradise, and made a promise to save each other a seat at Christ's banquet table. If Jorge's life was the only one to touch mine in all the weeks of prison ministry the balance would still tip to the positive, but he wasn't the only one, not by a long shot, he was just the first to laugh at my jokes.

Flowers & Arrows

William wore a hair shirt
somewhere around Italy,
shows you what I know about saints.

Little picture cards litter
the chaplain's desk,
flowers and arrows pierce the heart.

A yard and B yard assemblies,
melting pot of hot heads
and maimed spirits.

We gather to pray here,
two or more
the math of heaven.

Just a closer walk;
the forgiven getting up,
time after time, doing time.

We leave one chair open
for who went before,
and who comes after.

Each lost sheep
makes a sound only
the Shepherd can hear.

Chapter Three

A Ministry is Only a Hobby Until Someone Else Pitches In

The best way to call people into action is to make the action seem logical and inevitable. Giving up family time on a Sunday night week after week to visit convicts is not an automatic fill in the blank on anyone's church bulletin so I got creative. Our church had a top notch and growing praise music ministry due to the talent and anointing of our worship leader, Matt Blair. As the church grew, the need for additional musicians to support the second Sunday service led to an audition process.

I listened in at the auditions, hoping to find someone with a heart for praise music that wasn't quite up to par with the main service talent level, that might find leading a dozen inmates in worship a suitable calling. Pay dirt consisted of a young man about to enter military service who wanted some way to serve the Lord that would get him out of the house so he had one less night a week of his parents being nervous for his future.

The lad played guitar, or so he said, from the front row at chapel the following Sunday it was impossible to tell if he ever actually touched his strings and even less believable that the silent motions he made with his mouth was singing. Shyness had found a new champion. The inmates stood to clap along with the song and cheer out lyrics to whatever was in their heart at the time. The intermittent chorus swelled up to the front of the room and caught our guitar player like a sleeper wave. He raised his head just above the neck of his guitar and said, "Thank you." If the enthusiasm was something he generated it came from willingness, and not musical prowess, but it hooked him into returning week after week with song sheets of original tunes he wrote for the occasion.

Microphones helped him settle into being heard in the room, but being appreciated came from his nearly perfect attendance until it was time for him to be deployed. His entry into military service was buoyed by the wings of thirty or more chapel mates who came to know him as "Z" the guitar man. The confidence "Z" gained in playing before people was demonstrative, more especially so when he told me the chapel experience was the first time he ever played in public. He managed a return visit after about six months in the service and despite his new haircut, and the new muscles in his chest, the praise session picked up as if he had never left us, echoing Christ's promise to never leave or forsake us.

Our success in bringing in a musician encouraged me to seek some additional preachers and or prayer warriors to flesh out, or should I say Spirit out, the ministry team. The first such recruit was so positive and energetic, not to mention prepared, he had no less than thirty three by five cards with Scriptures he planned to use in his first talk. One would've been enough as just standing in front of the room reduced our 'speaker' into a sobbing mess. He proceeded to confess his sins in a manner more public than I had ever seen and knelt to ask the guys to pray for his repentance.

Half the room rushed forward to lay hands on the brother as he shook with the realization that the words of his mouth and the meditation of his heart were acceptable to the Lord and the entire chapel. Church had usually been a place where he had lost himself in the ups and downs of sermons and services, to find himself in the fulcrum of active faith left him with little recourse but to abandon his thoughtful preparation and rejoice in his new found fellowship. Years later when a severe health crisis struck his family his newly constructed unadulterated prayer life was a pillar against the storm.

Volunteering to minister to inmates seemed such an obvious opportunity to me I am often bewildered at the resistance and avoidance the issue seems to spark in people. The by now standard response of "God may be calling you to do that, but I haven't heard from Him," gave me chills the first time I heard it after approaching a friend of mine to join me. I'm not sure how that could be true if they were reading the same Gospel I was reading

(Matthew 25:36) but besides that, what would it hurt to take one Sunday night out of a year and just come by for a visit?

Certainly getting the paperwork together for security clearance can be a bit of a hassle and there is an uncomfortable threshold to cross the first time you step behind bars, but there is so much to be shared inside I don't know why the ratio of prison volunteers to Sunday school aides in most churches is less than one in a hundred or worse. Part of the reason I'm writing this account is to shed some light on a tucked away corner of Christian compassion in community. Regretfully I confess that if I ever learn to trust the Lord with the progress of Prison ministry in His church I will have learned something valuable indeed, until then, I'll keep turning over rocks, and look for responsive nuggets.

People often say where one door closes, another opens. The process of going through security gates takes this process literally. The first metal gate sounds a click and draws back allowing entrance into a holding cell. The second gate will not click until the first gate closes securely. It only takes a few seconds for the doors to co-ordinate, but for a few moments the sense of being a bull about to be released into the ring brings a smile. The power built up waiting for the gate is always in the Bible, not the person carrying it, but a quickening of spirit, an elation to purpose, a sort of shorthand version of Moses's glowing face after visiting with the Lord can illuminate a witnessing team.

It's not proper to skip across the yard, or draw any undue attention to yourself as you approach the inner security checks, but if it's true that we have such a great cloud of witnesses it must also be true that we can imagine, if not outright hear, their shouting as we bear light into darkness. This is not a predictable, automatic, nor readily audible event. Ordinary people don't get a movie score drumming up enthusiasm for the pace of their footsteps, yet I believe some of the adrenaline spike of walking past armed guards, maybe even garnering a friendly comment is as spiritual as it is chemical.

The Gospel going behind bars is as old as the Gospel itself, and as timeless. The letters Paul wrote from prison could be written and mailed today as legitimately as they were two thousand years ago. Back then they were delivered in person, and read aloud, from house to house, church to church, hospital ward to prison ward, person to person. This face to face encounter with believers eager for new information, eager for good news, is a common thread between today's prison ministries and the ministries of old. The shoes of the fisherman may have changed a bit since then but the blessing of peace that fall on the feet on the messengers is still the passport stamp of ambassadors for Christ.

Sometimes when I interview a first time visitor after service they'll mention a sense of timelessness; the hour plus wait for the inmates to be checked into chapel will blow by like a few minutes; or they'll talk about looking up inside the service as if they had dreamed of the visit years ago and the walls; or the songs and Scripture suddenly remind them of a missionary seed planted long ago in their spirit. I had an experience like that in Africa approaching a well where a woman was drawing water. One minute I was walking like my normal awkward self and with the next step I felt as if I had stepped into a movie set of The Living Bible.

The sensations, or sensationalism, of personal revelation can stir up a lot of conversation and confusion. I don't meant to pour any gas on that fire as much as to point out that joy is the currency of connection with the saints, living or gone ahead. If the joy of the Lord is our strength then feeling strong and joyful is the equipping He gives at each checkpoint in the process of entering His gates with praise.

When the Sanhedrin arrested Peter and John for healing a lame man in Solomon's Portico at the temple in Jerusalem they were questioned by what power or what name the apostles acted under since they recognized Peter and John as uneducated fisherman. Peter responded, "Rulers of the people and elders of the people: If this day we are judged for doing a good deed to a helpless man, and by what means he has been made well, let it be known to you, and to all the people of Israel, that by the name of Jesus Christ of Nazareth, whom you crucified, whom God raised from the dead, by Him this man stands before you whole (Acts 4:9-10)."

I like it that Peter characterizes his role in the miraculous healing as merely doing a good deed, I doubt the lame man saw it that way as he entered the temple-walking, leaping, and praising God. As my street savvy daughter would say when it comes to being a conduit for the Living Word, "You'd better recognize and ask someone." The simple act of volunteering to bring the Gospel into prison may be seen from the outside as merely doing a good deed, but from the eyes of the recipients, a visit can be miraculous.

Life locked in a block is already a lonesome thing, and with the threat of solitary confinement a very real daily possibility, any charitable contact with the outside world can be like manna from heaven. The temptation to think human connection is the extent of the experience minimizes divine exchange as the operative principle of ministry. It is much like saying Jesus was a great world teacher, but hardly the Son of God. Peter and John never stopped being simple fishermen even as they became great apostles.

Their simplicity confounded the Sanhedrin, comforted the growing church, and confirmed their testimony that they were with Him and acted solely in His name. We don't go into prison to entertain, as entertaining as we might be when we try to sing, or to enlighten as if we were some source of special insight or knowledge. Like Paul, we preach but one thing and that Christ crucified and resurrected. Revealed, reverent, and relevant are the three R's of ministry.

Most anyone can read stories about Jesus from the book, and it always helps to hear them, but to realize the steps taken to represent Him in prison are ordered by the Lord is a more pertinent and personal perspective. On the one hand Peter and John knew it could have been any one of the apostles that lifted the lame man to healing, but at the same time they must have marveled that is was them the Lord was working through. It is for such a time as this that we understand the answer to the prayer to create in us a clean heart and a willing spirit.

Walking across the yard to the chapel, escorted by a guard, or under the watchful eye of the tower, the scenery can be mostly internal. The sight of high walls, razor wire fences, forlorn attempts at landscaping, or even successful gardens tend to provoke a sense that if our lives had gone this way instead of that at some crucial junctures we could be the ones in state dungarees staring at the Bible thumpers coming down the lane.

Inmates are convicted criminals. In a maximum security prison like Pelican Bay they are all violent offenders. Compassion cannot cloud a minister's appreciation for the choices that led to incarceration, but the choice of what to do with the incarcerated time is where the fellowship of prison ministry aims to be productive. Serving a life sentenced saved is still serving a life sentence. The difference is in the quality of the service.

I'm not sure if prison administrators chart the positive effects of Gospel ministry. I know they let us in, usually graciously. One might hear an administrator give a grateful testimony at a banquet for volunteers, or get an enthusiastic handshake when gate passes are renewed, but the real recognition for anything achieved by volunteering will be next to our names in the Book of Life, and in the welcome we receive from inmates attending chapel.

Some will attend just to break routine, or to sit in a padded chair, but most will come because the presence of the Lord in lockup is the best hope for experiencing safety, a faithful sense of family, and being loved. Paul says in 1 Corinthians 13:13 "And now abide faith, hope, love, these three; but the greatest of these is love." Love is the deal. Love is the movement. Love is what remains. Love is what resurrects us, or to be theologically correct, love is Who resurrects us.

We ask people to 'have a heart' when we need mercy or forgiveness. Not having a heart for ministry is a phrase some people use to excuse themselves from a commitment to compassion, for a follower of Jesus it is not really an option. It is useful to consider that in prison ministry the compassion runs both ways, the inmates may care and pray for us as much as we do for them. In many institutions unless a volunteer comes in from the outside to lead them, worship services aren't part of the program.

I used to wear a button on my lapel that said "88% of life is just showing up." The percentage may be a little higher when it comes to getting chapel doors to open in lock down. The willingness to submit paperwork, gain clearance, follow procedure, and operate on a regimented schedule is rewarded when the inmates finally get checked in for service and share their appreciation with a handshake.

The greetings they give each other may be more intricate, animated, or humorous, but a face to face, man to man, connection is our mutual heritage in the kiss of Christ's peace. The quality of a sermon, the accuracy of a scriptural reference, the eloquence of an opening or closing prayer, all stem from the genuine fellowship extended in the first few minutes of getting together.

Consider the opening of so many of Paul's letters, "Grace, mercy, and peace from God our Father and Jesus Christ our Lord." 'Nuff said.

The Palm Before the Storm

Open hope in your hand
like ripe pomegranate
juice jewels,
open hope in your hand
like a cloth bound edition
with crisp dollars
between each ancient page.

Open hope in your hand
like the first bird's twitter
after a long night's rain,
open hope in your hand
like burst bean coffee scent, freshly ground
on a Saturday with no chores.

Open hope in your hand
like the buttons on a work shirt
after your shift,
open hope in your hand

like a door that takes both arms
against the wind.

Hope, is always in our hands.
Fists can't feel it.

Chapter Four

Throw Your Heart Hard and High

Leading a worship service in prison is a blast. People joke about being struck by a lightning bolt from heaven when they do something wrong, I think they have it backwards. The hairs on the back of your neck are likely to stand straight up the first time you face a truly convicted congregation. It is impossible for even the most staid individual on the planet not to get happy feet when a chorus of inmates begins a praise song like, "Wade in the Water" or "I'll Fly Away." The sense that Jesus has more joy for a person than normal life can offer is revealed in sliding left and clapping in time. If the family members praying for the inmates back home could see the church service begin to take off, "up in here" they'd cause an echo that would make angels bop and weave.

A lot of offenders had some church coming up. Some part of it that seemed unreachable then, seems unimpeachable now. The words might come back to memory, the melody ease a tightness in the neck born in adolescent anger, the clapping, the shout, the foot tapping are all steps of boldness toward the throne. No one forgets for a minute how we got to this place. The point is not to forget prison for a little while, but to remember deliverance for eternity.

Choosing a Scripture to build a service around can be as pragmatic as picking a topic such as idolatry and searching a concordance for relevant verses, a modern version might even include references to the NFL. Another approach might be to ask in prayer for an appropriate passage to 'jump off the page.' The tradition is to leave the selection to whomever is going to stand up in front of the room. I'd like to suggest that narrows the gate more than is necessary.

Hebrews 3:12 says, "Beware, brethren, lest there be in any of you an evil heart of unbelief in departing from the living God; but exhort one another daily, while it is called "Today," lest any of you be hardened through the deceitfulness of sin."

Exhort one another. It is imperative that the inmates be equipped as saints to exhort one another and encouraging them to bring a Scripture to mind for service is an excellent way to build confidence in the process.

And again in Hebrews 3:14 it says, "For we have become partakers of Christ if we hold the beginning of our confidence steadfast to the end, while it is said: "Today if you will hear His voice, do not harden your hearts as in the rebellion."

Making our hearts soft enough to receive His voice from an inmate fosters a culture of respectful attentiveness. We are charged with 'being ready in season and out' to defend the hope that is in us. This doesn't require an encyclopedic knowledge of Scripture that we might field any question or place any quote that comes up, but rather that by being examples of receptivity we can map out a progressive course by letting the Word be a lamp onto our feet.

The mutuality of our position as fellow worshipers is an enormous principle to communicate with the incarcerated. It puts the 'Our" into Our Father Who are in heaven. It was Jesus's claim that Sonship with the Father was His to claim and His to share that got Him crucified. The least we can do to live out that privilege is eliminate any sense of hierarchy in chapel services. That doesn't mean trying to fit in with the inmates by posturing or imitating their culture as much as adhering to the grace we share. Romans 3:22-24 says, "For there is no difference; for all have sinned and fall short of the Glory of God, being justified freely by His grace through the redemption that is in Christ Jesus,..."

It takes at least two steps to walk, one to come boldly before the throne of grace, and the other to humble yourself in the sight of the Lord. Inmates are expert, or at least very well schooled, in spotting phoniness. What you do for the least of these very much translates to the group as a whole. We are each of us the lost sheep covered by the Lamb, if we have confidence in that fact then that is the point where worship ought to take hold.

If, as is often the case when I prepare for a service, we wonder what in the world are we doing here, representing a Gospel of grace we barely recognize in our day to day experience, then we need to borrow on the foundation others have laid in our lives. Every man of God we've ever met, or heard speak, or have read about, is available through the Holy Spirit as a mentor, as an inspiration. That is the role we might fill for an inmate, or a protégé, if we credit Christ, and not ourselves, as the source of connection.

A word game we use that helps to illustrate this point is to vertically print out the letters E-G-O on a white board and fill in the space behind the letters to spell out Exit God's Order. The Holy Trinity is God the Father, God the Son, and The Holy Spirit. The unholy trinity is me, myself, and I. Crime, like sin, originates in the belief that every individual is different and separate from each other and thereby separable from God. Machismo believes it can hurt others without hurting itself.

Jesus invites a man, and of course that means ladies too, to Enter God's Order, to exhibit Good Orderly Direction, to learn from Him to be gentle, and to be humble in heart. Meeting inmates, mano a mano, in this spirit is where conversion and conversation take root. The good seed on good soil. One waters, another harvests, the brother in the jumpsuit could be your watering can as much as you might be his sword beat into a plowshare.

There are angels set among the guard towers. The cement rows of cellblocks house a temple rebuilt in three days. I've had volunteers remark after their first worship experience inside prison that they've been going to church their entire lives but never knew what a church service was meant to be until they praised God with inmates serving a life sentence.

Of course we were sentenced to death as soon as we were born. There is no escaping the physical fate of the body unless you happen to be lifted way up into the middle of the air like Elijah. Swing low sweet chariot and save a wretch like me makes a great medley but it is not an itinerary. Matthew 10:28 says, "And do not fear those who kill the body but cannot kill the soul. But rather fear Him who is able to destroy both soul and body in hell."

God is in the details. Matthew 10:38 says, "And he who does not take his cross and follow Me is not worthy of Me. He who finds his life will lose it, and he who loses his life for My sake will find it."

Our mortality is our cross. We carry it consciously, conscientiously, or not. His sake is the little children that He suffers to come unto him. Remember the apostles thought a crowd of little children pestering the Lord was a hindrance to true spirituality. They were wrong then, and they would be wrong now. Some become like little children to enter the kingdom, sometimes they wear DOC on their backs and take up the last chair in the room.

The word educate comes from *educare* , to bring up, draw out, to nurture. The use of Scripture in worship can easily slip into the cerebral, the historical, even the allegorical, but the Word is alive to discern the thoughts and intents of the heart. The Spirit circles the service, it needn't be as dramatic as the tongues of fire, but there is usually a soul or two anxious for the dove of peace to perch on their shoulder.

Maybe their smile is brighter then when they walked in the room, or maybe their eyes are brimming with tears they don't dare drop, maybe a passage has their head stuck on a page even as hidden wings flap behind their seat. Be aware, even eager to individualize the anointing of a service however briefly towards a particular brother's breakthrough. Just raising a hand to ask for prayer, clarification, or to give a praise report might be the act of courage that shakes a bond of unworthiness.

To walk out of a service changed is the goal for both the preacher and the preachee. Iron sharpens iron. Sometimes it softens as well.

The temptation is to teach, to show 'them' a thing or two about Scripture, to become, unwittingly perhaps, sons of the sorceress, showmen, superstars.

Even Jesus, rightfully called Teacher and Lord (John 13:13) set friend, not student, as an aspiration for the disciples. Friends learn things together, they share laterally, not from suggested positions of hierarchy. Being in front of a room carries the opportunity to be a vocal focal point, but the willingness to listen for how a message is received compared to seeking satisfaction in how it is delivered is what makes for reverential reference points for the attendees.

An inmate in a soft chair, like any churchgoer, has the tendency to doze off. After all Sunday is a day of rest. Sitting next to such a meditative spirit without raising a fuss might be the gentle touch of healing for a malcontent that could never sit still in a classroom or pew. The mind can only absorb what the rear end can endure, the same might be true of the heart and soul of a Sunday service. It is not just a sign of respect to have volunteers stand when they read Scripture during service, it also breaks the passive receptive tendencies of most worshipful gatherings.

An altar call is an obvious call to action in supernatural as well as natural realms. Jesus asks us to come to Him and then go make disciples, there isn't an escape clause that allows us to sit back and applaud the folks doing a better job of it than we are. In a non-incarcerated church we can delude ourselves into thinking we are supporting the spread of the Gospel by putting a check in the collection basket for missions. But the only way an inmate can spread the Gospel is to spread the Gospel.

St. Francis of Assisi prayed and lived to preach the Gospel wherever he went, but only when necessary to use words. Gaining confidence while protected in the church body has long been a training arena for expressing ability in a larger community. Interview a dozen Grammy winners and you'll find more than a handful that grew up singing in church. Ushering, greeting people, setting out chairs, a servant's heart is prepared by activity. Wisdom dictates that participation in the service imparts a sense of ownership in the proceedings which may in turn facilitate a truer sense of walking the walk than giving an ear to the pithy commentary of the speaker.

The first step in any journey maybe the longest one, but it is the second step that defines walking. "Tembe ya Jesu" is Swahili for "walk with Jesus". The subtle implication in this proverb is that "approaching the throne of grace with boldness (Hebrews 4:16)" only is the first step, but to "humble yourself under the mighty Hand of God (1Peter 5:6)" is what gives grace, movement, and direction to our testimony. The person most affected by a chapel service may not even be in the room but waiting back at the cell block to see if any of the things professed from the pulpit hold true on a stormy Monday.

Most of Paul's letters to the early believers begin with an expression of grace and peace from God the Father and the Lord Jesus Christ. First impressions are important and sometimes the only thing a person takes away from an exchange of ideas. We would do well to make grace and peace part of the toolkit we give inmates to guard their hearts.

Drawing men out of themselves into service by such simple acts as asking them to lead a prayer, or write prayer requests on a chalkboard, can heal some residue of ridicule, some potion of isolation that poisoned the man's sense of family and fellowship. Gang identification, the mob mentality, is the counterfeit of abiding in love. Perfect love casts out fear, violent demons jump the cliff at the sound of His voice. We, the sheep, know that voice and know that He calls us by name, and calls us friend. When the celestial telephone rings in our heart we must answer the call, hand the receiver to whomever is in the room with us and say, "It's for you."

Sometimes soliciting participation is a question of pouring gas on the fire or blowing on embers. The difference between coming to worship, versus merely attending a service, is usually apparent in body language, position in the room, or attention span. Certainly men who come prepared to worship need to be encouraged to do so, but not at the expense of attendees who may not be familiar, or comfortable, with an outgoing worship style.

The writer of Hebrews exhorts us to "Pursue peace with all people, and holiness, without which no one will see the Lord (Hebrews 12:14-15)." The early Christians bestowed a kiss of peace upon each other to signify their brotherhood in Christ. I'm not so sure that would fly inside prison, but a physical gesture, such as a hand shake, smile, eye contact, or a particularly un-funky dance move can go a long way in warming an indifferent attitude.

The perception of holiness as being something reserved for folks other than the 'normal' inmate is a lie from the pit of hell and needs to be extinguished by inclusion in the living waters of the Gospel. Flooding the men huddled in the corners of the room with attention might float their boat, sprinkling them with humor might draw them in, pouring praise and prayer into the service like a fire hose gone ballistic has its advantages, soaking the group in meditative song can certainly sprout seeds of change. The technique of inclusion doesn't matter as much as the intent.

Scripture says the soul pants for God as a deer might pant for water in a drought. (Psalm 42:1). Setting the stage for a convict to satisfy this longing in his soul, to drink in God's grace like a long, tall, cool glass of water is a main reason why we enter the gate. We prime the pump by imbibing in the cup of mercy for ourselves. Certainly private prayer in preparation of a prison visit is a reasonable sacrifice, but offering our example publicly can be instructionally beneficial.

Something as simple as leading the Lord's Prayer in a call and response format can smooth the way for a novice worshiper, as well as give old hands a tried and true handle on the pipeline of His presence. Worship is corporate and personal, it is public and private, it is what's up and what's going down. It is where we take our place with the angels, heads bowed and tattooed hands folded.

Chapter Five

Until a Real Apostle Shows Up, You're It

"How then shall they call on Him in whom they have not believed? And how shall they believe in Him of whom they have not heard? And how shall they hear without a preacher? And how shall they preach unless they are sent? As it is written:

"How beautiful are the feet of those who preach the Gospel of peace,

Who bring glad tidings of good things (Romans 10:14-15)!"

We have big shoes to fill when we take to a prison pulpit so it is nice to know our feet, or at least the steps we take to get there, are beautiful. Not a lot of people see themselves as capable of administering the Word to an assembly, let alone a room of violent offenders doing hard time. The fear of public speaking is one of the great phobias of our time. When Christ sent out the twelve He encouraged them saying, "Do not worry about how or what you should speak. For it will be given you in that hour what you should speak; for it is not you who speak, but the Spirit of your Father who speaks in you…Whatever I tell you in the dark, speak in the light: and what you hear in the ear, preach on the housetops (Matthew 10:19-20…27)."

Preaching the Gospel of peace is just that, nothing more, nothing less. Paul said in 1 Corinthians 2:2-4 "For I determined not to know anything among you except Jesus Christ and Him crucified. I was with you in weakness, in fear, and in much trembling. And my speech and my preaching were not with persuasive words of human wisdom, but in demonstration of the Spirit and of power, that your faith should not be in the wisdom of men but in the power of God."

Anecdotes, non-Scriptural references, life experiences, and personal insights are not forbidden in crafting a sermon if that is where the Spirit of your Father leads you. The best laid plans of men, and the most prepared stacks of note cards are often left untouched at the altar as the Holy Ghost directs the speaker toward the heart of the listener. Going against the grain of God from the podium can and will happen, a particularly personal revelation will be revealed as inconsequential, impertinent, or merely impossible to follow.

James tells it like it is, "We all stumble in many things. If any man does not stumble in word, he is a perfect man, able to bridle the whole body." James 3:2

The solution is to stumble forward. Admit immediately where we got off track, apologize for it, and apply for grace to get back in the groove. Jesus is the only perfect man, the rest of us must "show by good conduct that our efforts are done in the meekness of wisdom (James 3:13)." Convicts, maybe more so than most congregations, have carefully attuned antennas for deception, insincerity, and puffed up distraction. They want the Truth, and the Light, and won't sit still for us getting in the way of that.

Consequently the first change of heart the Gospel should effect is in ourselves. We know full well that a willing spirit, and not a wonderful vocabulary, is why we are called to preach. Learning that Paul's knees were knocking gives us a little room to move forward in our own jitters. When the butterflies begin to jump up in our stomach we can ask God to get them flying in formation and generate some enthusiasm for our message.

The very word, enthusiasm, comes from the Latin *enthusiasmus*, to be possessed by the Spirit. In my experience the notion that preaching needs to be dour, dogmatic, and disciplinary comes more from a need to be in control than from indwelling inspiration. Try to imagine Paul going on past midnight and returning to preach after reviving a lad that fell to his death from a window, it's not likely he was following a five point syllabus and just had to get to his synopsis.

Paul preached one thing; Christ crucified and resurrected. Remember, he didn't have the four Gospels to draw on; he had the light blind him on the road to persecuting Christians in Damascus, he had all his former training as a scholar of the Torah, which he considered as rubbish next to knowing Christ's suffering and triumph over sin and the grave, and he had whatever personal conviction and revelation he was gifted with by Jesus through the Holy Spirit.

On a missionary trip to Kenya our team leader was asked for stories about Jesus by a local craftsman, but "not from the book. I can read those for myself. What has Jesus done for you that can't be explained any other way." After sensing the sincerity of the request the leader responded, "He has brought me here to meet you." The international fellowship that hatched from this direct exchange bears such eternal consequence.

To be mindful of eternal consequence does wonders in focusing a preacher's ability to be real, relevant, and revelatory. "What do you think? If a man has a hundred sheep, and one of them goes astray, does he not leave the ninety-nine and go to the mountains to seek the one that is straying? And if he finds it, assuredly, I say to you, he rejoices more over that sheep than over the ninety-nine that did not go astray (Matthew 18:12-13)."

Rejoicing adds a particular quality to a speaker's voice, it puts extra 'ups', "mad hops" in one's jump, rejoicing lets a listener know they came just in time for the good parts, rejoicing aligns one's heart with heaven, with all the trees of the wood, and the multitude of isles (Psalm 96:11-12, Psalm 97:1).

Rejoicing is a specific instruction to the brethren charged with bearing Christ's light into darkness. "Rejoice in the Lord, always. Again I say rejoice (Philippians 4:4)." "Jesus is the same yesterday, today, and tomorrow. Do not be carried about with various and strange doctrines (Hebrews 13:8-9)." The Gospel of peace is never old hat. It doesn't need spicing up, or seasoning. Causing every head to bow, every knee to bend, and every tongue to confess the name of Jesus would be quite the sufficient sermon and service.

It is that Spirit that we wish to foster in our talk and in our walk. We often allow such reverence to enter into our praise singing and then turn around and discard it in the belief that preaching needs to be more pragmatic, as if there is anything in this world, or the next, more practical than partaking in His holiness.

Putting the Word into words isn't a matter of diction or cadence. Connection comes in being receptive to the Spirit's leading, and respectful of the attendees attention span. Incarcerated congregations are, usually, a mix of cultures. A bombastic thunder throated style might resonate with a portion of the group and leave the other members crossing their arms and rolling their eyes. Consequently a speaker without the power of conviction is likely to find a chorus of snores drowning the finer points of the sermon.

The style of the message, and the messenger, ought always point to Christ like iron filings responding to a magnet. "And I, brethren, when I came to you, did not come with excellence of speech, or of wisdom, declaring to you the testimony of God (1 Corinthians 2:1)." Placing ourselves on the hill for the Sermon on the Mount, or in the boat as He calmed the waves is the desire of our hearts and the best focal point of addressing an assembly of God. It is the finished work of Jesus that we work with; we may never know how much it cost, to see our sins upon that cross, but we can approximate.

Paul bemoaned not being able to speak to his audience as spiritual people but as mere babes in Christ (1 Corinthians 3:1) while Peter exhorts us as newborn babes to desire the pure milk of the Word. (1Peter 2:1) Every gathering will have a range of Gospel experience and a spectrum of grace consciousness. The more mature believer may well help the novice find their place in Scripture and the more mature worship leader will encourage partnership in unpacking the interpretation of particular passages.

The tonality of a meeting, the timbre of insights offered for consideration, and the vibrancy of comprehension all communicate to a place in the heart that nurtures the planted seed long after the service has been dismissed. A mentor of mine said the quality of his manners, the strength of his handshake, and the gentleness of his spirit carried the Gospel further and truer than any sermon he prepared, or delivered, no matter the number of note cards, footnotes, or relevant power points.

We look to serve the lost sheep, to urge them along the true path. If all we can follow is our nose, let us aim to sniff the incense that ascends before God from the hand of the angels, along with the prayers of the saints. A speaker need not find one voice to pray in and another for preaching. Breaking into prayer, or praise, is like finding a blueberry as the proof of the pudding.

We deliver ourselves as living epistles. Showing up to preach in prison speaks to the heart of the matter before we even utter a word. We go out of our way to make the Way clearer. Before the Lamb of God was revealed to John the Baptist he said, "I am the voice of one crying in the wilderness: Make straight the way of the Lord (John 1:23)." He was quoting Isaiah's 'comfort speech' in chapter forty; "The glory of the Lord shall be revealed, all flesh shall see it together; for the mouth of the Lord has spoken.

The voice said, "Cry out!" and the man answered, "What shall I cry?"

All flesh is grass, and all its loveliness is like the flower of the field. The grass withers, the flower fades, because the breath of the Lord blows upon it; surely the people are grass. The grass withers, the flower fades, but the word of our God stands forever (Isaiah 40 5-8)."

As long as men have been called out to speak to the faithful, or even the unfaithful for that matter, they have been directed to point out the advantage of the eternal over the temporal. Paul echoes this perspective in 2 Corinthians 15-18 "For all things are for your sakes, that grace, having spread through the many, may cause thanksgiving to abound to the glory of God.

Therefore we do not lose heart. Even though our outward man is perishing, yet the inward man is being renewed day by day. For our light affliction, which is but for a moment, is working for us a far more exceeding and eternal weight of glory, while we do not look at the things which are seen, but at the things which are not seen. For the things which are seen are temporary, but the things which are not seen are eternal."

To spread grace through the yard we speak grace in the chapel. "But where sin abounded, grace abounded much more... (Romans 5:20)." The attitude of the world toward life behind bars is that sin certainly abounds there. The world would like to believe that sin can be contained by thick walls and barbed wire, but sin is contained, if that's the right word, in the hearts and minds of men. Light casts out darkness, perfect love casts out fear, and grace dissipates sin and condemnation. Jesus rolled away the stone from the entrance to the tomb, the ultimate 'solitary confinement'. He has no trouble penetrating walls, locked doors, even dungeons, but He will only enter a heart by invitation.

Men of faith must be trained to trust that, to trust that and learn more about the Gentleman of Heaven's plans for them. "For I Know the thoughts that I think toward you, says the Lord, thoughts of peace and not of evil, to give you a future and a hope (Jeremiah 29:11." Who is more unlikely to perceive a future of hope and peace than an incarcerated criminal? And what lost sheep might the Lord most desire to bring into His fold, this Lord who died for us while we were yet sinners?

It may be helpful to consider doubt as a breeding ground for faith. If we know a thing, how can we hope it is true, it either is or it isn't. "God so loved the world That He gave His only Son... (John 3:16)." There is a lot to digest just in the first half of this famous Scripture. Familiarity with this verse, so often waved on a cardboard sign behind home plate for the TV cameras, might cause us to diminish the magnitude of God giving us His Son because He so loved us.

When we give a gift it is out of our hands; the radio controlled car sits in the closet of the nine year old boy just days after the excitement of tearing through the gift wrap expires, the Christmas sweater stays packed in the bottom of the drawer until next December. We say it is the thought that counts because we know we won't always use, or actually appreciate the gift.

God nearly says the same thing. Here is my Son, do with Him what you will; ignore Him, abuse him, murder Him, follow Him, adore Him. The choice is ours.

Even as we choose to bring the Gospel of peace and grace inside prison walls we must remember how close we are at any moment to ignoring Christ's example and thinking the call to ministry has something to do with our skill set.

The doubt that He could run His Kingdom without us gives way to the faith that if He could use a talking donkey there might be a place for us in His purpose. The place for us in His purpose is an excellent, universal, and perpetual topic for any sermon, especially in prison. "Then those who feared the Lord spoke to one another, and the Lord listened and heard them; so a book of remembrance was written before Him for those who fear the

Lord, who revere him and meditate on His name. "

"They shall be mine," says the Lord of hosts, "on that day I will make them my jewels, my special treasure. And I will spare them as a man spares his own son. Then there shall again be discernment between the righteous and the wicked, between those who serve the lord and those who do not serve (Malachi 4:16-18)."

Note that those that feared the Lord spoke to one another. A sermon need not be a one way communication, at its best it is a conversation, held in the hearing of the Lord.

Groan

Dawn at the Klamath,

a twelve point elk struts among deer mossed
stumps

as the Yurok's golden bear guards the new
bridge,

already under repair.

After practicing my chaplain ID smile

in the rearview mirror,

I receive the nod of the flagmen

and renew my drive to prison.

In a few miles, the forest,

and the mountains too,

will give way to thousands

of cement blocks,

and light, not the yellow sun streaming
through

redwoods and firs, will blink

florescent as the state budget allows.

It's the most natural thing in the world,
poetically,

politically, to ignore caged humans in these
parts

and laud wild animals,

but quit the ignition, and listen at the gate;

all creation groans

for the re-birth of our sons doing time.

Lend an ear to the wilderness crying

from a housing unit

never meant to be called home.

Chapter Six

I Pray the Lord My Soul to Keep

The unbelieving world asks, "What good is prayer?" never guessing what evil has been prevented, or diminished by the unseen efforts of petitioning saints. A popular novel of the seventies, "Jonathon Livingston Seagull" made an argument that if you argue for your limitations, they're yours. Campaigning against the effectiveness of prayer is a sure fire way to disprove its place in a person's life, but it will not unseat prayer as a hinge of creation.

When God created all that is made from what is unmade, He spoke it into existence. He imagined it and brought it forth by speech. He prayed every bit of every it that there is into reality, and when He made us He made us in His own image. He gave us, and us alone, imagination and speech. We were made to communicate, to perceive, to ascertain. Would it stand to reason that our Maker would make us capable of communicating, of worshipping, with Him in Spirit and in Truth? Reasoning may be the wrong track to train our thoughts. We are told to "trust the Lord with all our heart and lean not on our own understanding (Proverb 3:5)."

Prayer is an act of faith. When Jonathon prayed before battle he said 'perhaps' the Lord would deliver the Philistines into his hand, when Jesus prayed He said "I know You have heard me." The one time Jesus's righteous anger was recorded He drove the money changers from the temple saying, "Is it not written, "My house shall be called a house of prayer for all nations?" But you have made it a den of thieves (Mark 11:17)."

Entering into prison ministry we reverse that curse. We come into a den of thieves intent on resurrecting it into a house of prayer. I'm not a craftsman, if I need to fix something around the house I pick up the phone and call somebody qualified to git-r-done. I sometimes watch these miracle makers prepare to make a repair. Assess the problem, choose the right tool, lay out the materials, make a plan, and do the next right thing until the job is completed.

That's how prayer works. We call in the supernaturally qualified, we cast our cares, unseen forces come to bear and we do the next right thing. We prepare for the supernatural repairing of our world, until Jesus comes, by prayer. A beginner's prayer might well be just a hope to see the face between time and space, a simple, "Are you there, God?" The despondent may cry for help, for unfathomable deliverance; the weary for rest, the weak for strength, the ill for healing, the wealthy for usefulness, the talented for collaboration, the isolated for companionship, the violent for calmness, or the irreverent for depth of meaning.

Prayers outpoint the stars, they baffle the intricacy of snowflakes as if they were paper cutouts in a kindergarten, they wash troubled waters until they still. Prayer brings drops from clouds of doubt to the most parched affection, prayer sometimes settles the storm, sometimes, the sailor. Praying is our life's work. The apostles may have asked Jesus for a thousand favors or blessings we'll never hear about, but what we know is, they asked Him to teach them to pray.

We ask for the same thing going into jail and we ask to learn more about praying by praying in community, by discussion, by searching Scripture, by example, by receiving, and respecting praise reports. Prayer is personal, of course, but it can also be intercessory. Learning to pray for others, especially unbelievers, can be a supernatural application of the time served behind bars to free souls from the accusing grip of Satan.

"Without faith it is impossible to please him, for he who comes to God must believe that He is, and that he is a rewarded of those who urgently seek Him (Hebrews 11:6)." One such reward is answered prayer, but another reward is the privilege of being called to prayer in the first place. As Christians we don't rely on loudspeakers, or recorded mullahs and militant peer pressure, to get us to our knees. Hopefully, and I mean that literally, we respond to that still small voice that asks, "Won't you join me in consideration of My grace being sufficient?"

On a mission trip to Costa Rica to build a refuge campus for persecuted pastors a group of us gathered for prayer before hitting the shovels and stacks of drainage tiles we needed to install before rainy season. A circle of believers, in service, asked to pray. What could be more natural than missionary men standing with their heads bowed? As per normal, someone asked for someone to lead us in prayer, and as per normal, everyman there deferred.

Since drawing straws, or casting lots seemed a bit over the top we nominated a man who had not yet led us in prayer that week. Isaiah declared himself a man of unclean lips, a man undone when God called him to speak in His name. Jeremiah protested that he was too young to speak, and Ezekiel fell on his face to the ground when put in the same position, but none of them likely revealed the terror of our friend's face at the prospect of putting together a vocal prayer.

We constructed classrooms in that week, embanked roads against erosion, and planted scores of coconut trees, but the greatest miracle we saw during that trip was this man's decision to come right out and say, "Our Father, who art in heaven..." A real problem with taking the ability to pray for granted is that the prayers themselves are less likely to be granted if we're ho hum about the honor of calling upon the living God of the universe. Once our friend realized his reverence for the Lord wouldn't be put into jeopardy by his diction, or word choice, he was able to intercede for our success in completing our project.

Guiding someone, especially someone shy, or browbeaten, into prayer falls close to the adage about teaching a man to fish instead of taking him to McDonald's. If you ask any bunch of guys who is the "best" at prayer in their midst you are likely to get an answer, and it will never be the guy responding. Most men, whether incarcerated or not, just won't picture themselves as being prayer people, let alone becoming a prayer warrior. The possibility must precede the discipline and our personal accounting of how we've learned to pray can be a roadmap to a very precious journey.

Few people would take issue with encouraging others to pray, and fewer people still will actually engage in one on one, folded hand to folded hand, encouragement. Without making a parlor game out of the experience we have incorporated time for soft or silent prayer exchanges. Random partners are asked to push their chairs together and talk about prayer requests, prayer experiences, praying people they have known, or scriptural prayer references as a gathering together in preparation for praying for each other.

For many men sitting face to face and being expected to pray is more like being on the hot seat than being in the mercy seat, but you play like you practice, so the exercise will almost always have value. Some guys take to it like a thoroughbred rounding the back stretch and others resemble a turtle measuring the change in atmospheric pressure by wrinkling his nose. It may come down to just swapping names and inviting the Lord into the mix, "Jesus take care of Jimmy. Jesus look upon John."

Covering a brother's family in prayer can weave a type of security into inmates relationships with each other. It's not likely that any family situations brought into the prayer circle are going to be strange or shocking to any of the participants joined in prayer. The problems incarceration brings to families are more in common than unique, bringing them to the altar ranks among the most redemptive things an inmate can do with his time served.

We encourage inmates to become silent intercessors. The fledgling prayer cub picks someone he interacts with, or at least can observe, who is the least likely to be praying themselves, or even have anyone else praying for them, and begin a twenty one day silent prayer campaign in the subject person's behalf. The reports that come back range from a whole lot of nothing happened to stories of strange smiles, unexpected acts of consideration, sudden connections, even sparks of spiritual curiosity.

Receiving updates on prayer campaigns, whether they are private, or corporate, fuels the fire of faith that warms our upraised hands. It is helpful to visualize prayer as an ocean with wave after wave coming into our shore and pulling bits of the beach into tidal circulation and bringing prizes of driftwood and exotic shells in exchange. Of course the actual mechanism of prayer is supernatural and defies even the most eloquent explanation, but to sense it as an ongoing inhalation and exhalation we share with the Creator who breathed His life into us comes pretty close to a universal perspective.

"Then that same day at evening, being the first day of the week, when the doors were shut where the disciples were assembled for fear of the Jews, Jesus came and stood in the midst, and said to them, "Peace be with you." When He said this He showed them His hands and His side. Then the disciples were glad when they saw the Lord. So Jesus said to them again, "Peace be to you! As the Father has sent Me, I also send you." And when He had said this He breathed on them and said, "Receive the Holy Spirit (John 20:19-22)."

Receiving the peace of Christ is the reward, the payoff of prayer. The healing requested may or may not manifest, the needed guidance may be plain and planned, or delayed, the perspective gained or lost, the position moved into or missed by a mile. The physical proof, the signs and wonders that an unbelieving generation clamors for are not notches on the prayer slinger's gun, yet praying people all speak of prayers answered. And speaking of them within the confines of a safe group of purpose driven men puts bricks in the wall of the temple we aim to make of our lives.

If a man can learn how to cuss he can learn to pray. My pastor liked to point out that Peter cursed aloud when he denied Christ. He called it praying like a sailor. Playing the B-side. "When He had called the multitude to Himself, He said to them, "Hear and understand: Not what goes into the mouth defiles a man; but what comes out of the mouth, this defiles a man...for out of the heart proceed evil thoughts, murders, adulteries, fornications, thefts, false witness, blasphemies (Matthew 15:11...19)."

David knew what his heart was capable of expressing when he cried out in Psalm 51, "Create in me a clean heart, O God, and renew a steadfast spirit within me...Deliver me from bloodguilt, O God, the God of my salvation, and my tongue shall sing aloud of Your righteousness. O Lord, open my lips, and my mouth shall show forth Your praise."

Many a bluff is brought up short with the challenge to 'put your money where your mouth is.' Prayer is how we lay our cards on the table. Habit and discipline play some part in developing a prayer life. We need tools to convert the perversion of wringing our hands in worry to folding them in prayer. Fellowship, brotherhood, accountability partners, the joining of my prayer life to yours strengthens the weave. "Though one may be overcome by another, two can withstand him. And a threefold cord is not quickly broken (Ecclesiastes 4:12)."

The Oscar winning movie, "Gravity" has a scene in which the protagonist is alone in space, fearing her end, and sensing prayer is her only hope, despairs that no one ever taught her how to pray. If we do nothing but give the example of how we learned to pray we may fill a gap in a prisoner's life as deep as all of space.

Black holes are not limited to just the cosmos, the implosion of a soul without hope can suck the life from a person as surely as the lack of matter and mass can mess with the most precise equation of the universe.

"Let the word of Christ dwell in you richly in all wisdom, teaching and admonishing one another in psalms and hymns and spiritual songs, singing with grace in your hearts to the Lord (Colossians 3: 16)." We are to teach. I don't know if my singing voice is the best vehicle for that, I tend to bend some notes in a hill-billy way that I have no claim to, but the sincerity of wanting to pass on what has been passed on to us can seem like music to those that are hungry for compassion and understanding.

As it says in Colossians 3:8, we are to put off the old man: anger, malice, blasphemy, filthy language and put on the new: tender mercies, kindness, humility, meekness, longsuffering; bearing with one another, forgiving one another even as Christ forgave. This is a tall order and breaking it down into a single prayer for a single step forward, forgiving as Christ forgave, toward a particular person can be a foot in the door of a new perspective. "Jesus help me forgive_____ ." might be as much spiritual growth as an inmate, or any of us, needs for his entire time inside.

There is a story of three holy men who lived simple lives in isolation on an island in the Aegean Sea. Many healings were attributed to their concern for the fishermen in the surrounding area. A local bishop decided to investigate and after rowing across to see them was appalled at their lack of scriptural knowledge and proceeded to instruct them into proper theology including The Lord's

Prayer. Satisfied that he had succeeded in correcting the hermits he sailed off for the mainland only to see his boat followed by a blinding light. It was the saints running across the waves.

"Bishop! Bishop!" they cried. "We have forgotten the prayer you taught us, please teach us again."

The astonished bishop asked them how they managed to catch up to his boat.

"We prayed, "God, You are Three, we are three, have mercy on us." And hurried to catch you."

The bishop, humbled in the boat, bid them return to the island and continue living as they had been, and to pray for him to understand the power and purity of their prayer.

As with person to person communication, prayer is not a matter of what you say as much as how you say it. God searches the heart, not the word play or style, some folks punctuate their prayer cadence by throwing in the phrase "Father-God" much like Max Roach rides his high hat in a drum solo, some folks moan a few decibels lower than their normal speaking voices, other people break into "tongues' which usually mimic some sort of Semetic phonetics. Paul says in Romans 8:26 "For we do not know what we should pray for as we ought, but the Spirit Himself makes intercession for us with groanings that can't be uttered."

Jesus tells the parable in Luke 18:9-14 of two men standing to pray in the temple. He spoke this parable to some who trusted in themselves that they were righteous and despised others: "Two men went up to the temple to pray, one a Pharisee and the other a tax collector. The Pharisee stood and prayed thus with himself, "God, I thank you that I am not like other men; extortioners, unjust, adulterers, or even as this tax collector. I fast twice a week; I give tithes of all I possess." The tax collector, standing afar off, would not so much as raise his eyes to heaven, but beat his breast, saying, "God, be merciful to me a sinner!" I tell you this man went down to his house justified rather than the other; for everyone who exalts himself will be humbled, and he who humbles himself will be exalted."

The stages of grief that went through me after my father passed away left me without a prayer language, other than tears, for quite a while. One day I realized that the core prayer, the foundation of all the praying I'd ever done, came from the prayer I'd heard him say at the dinner table, "Bless us O Lord, and these Thy gifts, which we receive from Thy bounty, through Christ, Our Lord. Amen." I began to repeat it, almost as a mantra, and came back to a hope and a trust that the best is yet to come. Keep It Simple Saints. Prayer is an action, not an act, and actions, as we all know, speak louder than words.

Read It and Weave

If the sun on my back
had fingernails,
if the wind whistled in the Dorian mode,
if the kindness of paper to my pen
could sing, then
my good foot would climb goat sure
the rock wall and my garden ticket,
creased
and thumbed, allow the guards
to open the gates
of Pelican Bay State Prison.

But the hunger strike, these fifty days,
avoids light, masks the iron shadow
and confines all to a windowless
warp of the soul.

"No one lights a lamp
and sets it under a basket...'

but if you lift even a lip of the woven
stories

there is light enough,

to read.

Chapter Seven

Love Up in The Middle of The Air

Prison ministry is my life's work. I don't get paid for it, nor do I get to do it very often. I average 2 hours a month. Over the years at San Quentin State Prison, New Hanover County Department of Corrections, and currently at Pelican Bay Maximum Security state Prison I've made nearly 200 visits. The joke I make with inmates is I've been going to prison more often than any of them, difference being of course is I get to leave. But the joke is on me because the connections I've made with the men inside never leave me.

What the men have done to get locked up is none of my business; encouraging them to make a difference, to be a positive example, to be Kingdom Builders is the bottom line. Each venture inside ought to add to the spiritual stature of the assembled. The building blocks we use are living stones of belief stacked together to make heart felt walls, to repair the kind of fences and hedges that make good neighbors. We make straight the path to realize that we are indeed the blood bought brothers that Christ died to forgive.

We take a certain Scripture, Matthew 3:17, as a starting point for a new legacy, a new lineage. In the story Jesus has just been baptized by John and "suddenly a Voice came from heaven, saying, "This is my beloved Son, in whom I am well pleased." The chance that an inmate has ever felt that he was a beloved son in whom anyone was ever well pleased is remote to the point of infinitesimal. As we take the beginning of the Lord's Prayer, calling out "Abba Father" as a definition of who we are; brothers in Christ, children of God, we can extend the 'family resemblance' to claim that we are each beloved sons in whom God is well pleased.

The BSG Gang. The Beloved Sons of God Gang. We don't have a handshake as yet, and the only sign we throw down is the sign of the cross. Our sole activity is to accept, if only for as long as it takes to say it out loud, that we are beloved of God. Part of our re-identification process is to examine how despised Jesus was in His time on earth, to consider the contempt, even today, that identifying with Christ can bring. Jesus lowered himself from heaven just to become human, but hardly stopped there. He accepted the ridicule that came along with being a Nazarene, "from the wrong side of the tracks" years before tracks were invented. He was obedient even onto the cross. He had nowhere to lay his head.

At each point along the redemption story Christ lowered Himself to exalt us. We who are worth more than many sparrows, to put it lightly, can rise up, renewed like the eagle, because it is God's desire and purpose that we meet Him there in the middle of the rarified air of freedom from condemnation. The life work of the inmate, the ministry of those ministered to, is our measure, shaken down and pressed together.

My Pastor assisted seven life term serving inmates into getting paroled. Six of them are full time ministers and pastors today. He began his ministry by sitting with one inmate for hours on end because he recognized the real prison operating in the convict's life was loneliness.

Pastor Wesley taught him the most important rule to follow when dealing with distraught people was the 3H rule. Hug-Hush-Hang out. The quality of time spent in service begins with comforting and grows towards courage.

It's difficult, maybe even beyond our reach to get someone to believe something, but it is a divine privilege to be with them when they get it, when they gain the perspective that they are beloved and well pleasing to the Father because they believe in His Son's sacrifice and victory on their behalf. It is said there is much rejoicing in heaven when a sinner repents, we do a pretty fair job of raising a righteous ruckus when we recognize the light in a convict's eyes as being His, the Light of the world.

This recognition stems from discerning the difference between critical thinking versus having a critical attitude. Paul says in Romans 12:3 we are "… not to think of himself more highly than he ought, but to think soberly, as God has dealt to each one a measure of faith." The obvious extreme of making ourselves taller by cutting others down is pretty easy to define, but the inverse, cutting ourselves down with a false humility, is equally off the mark of thinking soberly.

God thinks us worthy of redemption. The Accuser of the Brethren begs to differ. There is no other storyline in the heavenlies.

On this side of the grave philosophies abound that there is no need of redemption, that things are just fine, or just futile, the way things are. The "eat, drink, and be merry, for tomorrow we die" crowd likes to take this bit of Ecclesiastes to heart as if it is the whole story, but the writer himself finishes the book with; "Let us hear the conclusion of the whole matter: Fear God and keep His commandments, for this is man's all. For God will bring every work into judgment, including every secret thing, whether good or evil."

Our work, inside the walls and out, is to "love the Lord your God and to love your neighbor as yourself (Matthew 22:34-40)." The exchange of ideas that moves us along the line of loving God, rather than 'merely' fearing and respecting Him, is ministry. One of our favorite hymns to sing at chapel is "Love Me Tender" which has a similar chord structure to "Amazing Grace" and makes for a sweet medley and profound understanding of what being in the plan, and the presence, of the Lord entails.

"If you love Me, you will keep My commandments (John 14:15)." At first glance this seems a reprimand until we search out that Jesus's commands were "to love the Lord your

God with all your heart, mind, and strength; and to love your neighbor as yourself (Matthew 22:34)." But can love be conjured up in response to a directive, even a divine one?

It may serve a human purpose to think God so fickle and conditional but Scripture reminds us that "God demonstrates His own love towards us, in that while we were yet sinners, Christ died for us (Romans 5:8)." Our ability to reason, especially when it comes to things divine, is hampered by our experience and imagination. It is one reason Scripture counsels us, "not to lean on our own understanding (Proverbs 3:5)." There is however no restriction on stretching our minds and hearts to try and engage with the wisdom that love reveals.

Love isn't just the centerpiece, it is the whole foundation of our faith. "If we love one another, God abides in us, and His love has been perfected in us." I don't often 'feel' perfected in love. I get afraid. John says, "There is no fear in love; but perfect love casts out fear, because love involves torment." 1John 4:18 Earlier in the same epistle he says, "And we have known and believed the love God has for us (1 John 4:16)." The implication is knowing we are loved is one thing, believing we are loved, is another. It is the core of all prayer, all fellowship, all worship, all ministry, all testimony.

Paul begins every letter he wrote to the early church with the greeting; "Grace to you and peace from God our Father and the Lord Jesus Christ." In a way he needn't add another word and his message would still be complete. Grace is the gift, peace the result. The gift of presence in prison ministry is more of the story than we who go in and out realize. Taking the time, making the effort to go inside the bars and just sit side by side with locked up men, is as much a message as anything that comes from a pulpit.

An inmate's family may not be able to afford the gas, or even have the inclination, to visit very often. God Himself thought loneliness and isolation such a devastating predicament that He begot His Son, and sent Him to us, as a guarantee that He "would never leave us, nor forsake us (Hebrews 13:5)." At the time of this writing the number of scheduled volunteer chaplain visits at Pelican Bay Maximum Security State Prison in California is 36/year. A chapel service is considered large if it brings in 30 inmates out of 3,000 in residence. There is some serious forsaking to be overcome.

When I first approached the administration at the prison about beginning a ministry they asked me who told me to call them. Being a quick witted zealot I replied, "God." I got my appointment.

Often when I speak at a church I'm approached by people who are very appreciative of prison ministries in theory, but "just don't feel they are called" to go inside. In the early days I took offense and muttered to myself that their Bibles must be a few pages short, but who knows, they may be right. Even Jesus said, "He who has ears, let him hear." Matthew 11:15

Maybe there is something special about people who answer the call. That's not been my experience, if anything it is the ordinary who are ordained. The well-worn phrase, "There but for the grace of God go I" might be re-written to say, "There because of the grace of God go I" when it comes to jail house revival.

Chances are good your community or your church already has established ministries. Seek and you shall find. Anyone going in will be glad to talk to you. Maybe your best service is to support existing programs as a prayer intercessor, or to pay for an occasional breakfast and chat, or supply Bibles, or gas money for transport. Find a need and fill it, the least that could happen is you'll make a friend.

There's always something to do, up until now there hasn't always been someone willing to do it, but now there is, maybe you've already begun to work it out, that someone could be you.

Graffito

Elk stands,
mallard roosts,
a big lagoon
named Big Lagoon,
the drive to Pelican Bay State
Prison.

The boys have tattooed heads
and necks,
insignia knuckles,
state issued pants as low as gravity
and code permits.

Forgive Us Christ King
is carved in the plaster chapel wall,
grammatical rescue, sound
theology.

A sleeping Villa Boy
startles to join the choir,
mercy chasing all the days of his life.

His forgiving heart
slips eternity
past the guards.

Chapter Eight

Mano` a Mano`

Because of movie and media references most of us have an image or idea about solitary confinement. Still it would be less foreign to most of us to shrink to the size of an insect and be escorted through an ant colony than it is to enter the Secure Housing Unit at Pelican Bay State Prison. There are court cases reviewing the legality and, by inference, the humanity of the facility and the policies that guide its operation. There are political contentions and psychological research papers aplenty. The quality of life in the SHU is the primary reason the United Nations considers Pelican Bay to be among the ten worst prisons in the world.

Visiting inmates in Secure Housing Units requires a brand new set of rules, such as, "Don't get within spitting distance." Since the advent of AIDS, any contact with severely restricted inmates is considered life threatening to the visitor. "Make sure your hands are visible at all times. Don't maintain eye contact for more than a few seconds as it may be construed as a stare down."

The instructional advice given during an orientation tour of SHU is designed to weed out the curious from the curate. A visit is always monitored by multiple cameras, and violating something as seemingly innocent as maintaining a three-foot distance between inmate and minister can shut it down. A public conversation requires the inmate to leave his cell, shackled wrists to ankles, and be escorted the ten feet from his cell door to a common area where he can speak with a visitor through a six-inch metal cage.

A semi-private type of pastoral care visit, such as administering communion, would require the minister to enter the common area and approach the inmate's cell. A private consultation, such as hearing confession, preparing for an inmate's wedding, or informing of a death in the family, is conducted in a "wet cell," so named because the inmate will go through a supervised showering, as well as a cavity search and evacuation.

A visit can only be initiated by the inmate, and then only if the prisoner has a named contact person with the appropriate security clearance to call upon. Unless an inmate who is already familiar with a minister through chapel services gets sent to secure housing, there is little opportunity to build a connection.

Including folks we may never meet in our prayer life might be the most impact we ever have on lives in the hole. Secure housing is designed to frustrate every effort or desire for human, let alone divine, contact. At Pelican Bay State Prison, as much as half the population is incarcerated in SHU, and the average confinement period is upward of four years.

Grace is the only key to unlock the bitterness, resentment, and isolation that works to strangle us. Whether it is an inmate's heart, or our own that is bound up, it is Jesus, and Jesus alone, that breaks every chain of the soul … especially when the minister is the weakest link. Our teams first visit inside was the result of a scheduling foul up. One of our normal chapel services was too late getting started and a special guest speaker was booked for the other yard. The chaplain saw an opportunity where we saw crisis and invited two of us to join him as he made his rounds in SHU.

We arrived at the first gate, received our protective body armor and said good bye to natural lighting. The corridor to the next gate bent a few directions, emergency exit arrows on the ceiling seemed to indicate that going further inside the building was going the wrong way. The blocks are divided alphabetically by degree of danger. Some inmates are inside to protect them from gang retaliation, most are there for what the authorities perceive as active gang affiliations or for violent infractions on the yard.

The second gate is encased in bullet proof glass. One guard monitored the sign-in book, the other stand guard, weapon in hand. Another run of echoing florescent lit corridors brought us to the blocks and the double caged doors. As our visit was rather impromptu we arrived inconveniently at shift change and had to wait beneath the see through turret for the check and recheck of every lock and key of the interior doors to the actual housing units. We were quiet, the cells were not. The chaplain had forty-five minutes allotted to visit. The wait took twenty. The guards weren't chatty, or flexible.

The keys finally opened the interior cage and we faced the housing row. Two stories high. Five cells wide. Lower floor, two inmates to a cell. Upper floor, one. I couldn't estimate the exact dimensions but if an inmate wanted to scratch his back he'd likely have to negotiate space with his cellie. Underwear was hung to dry between the sink and toilet, each bunk had a shelf for four books and the walls had photos that passed for family. The guard unlocked a small flap on the door and, after inspecting the New Testaments we brought with us for contraband, allowed us to pass the Good News to some very eager hands.

The hands that took my gift were white and young. Twenty three months in so far, no end in sight. When time is an unmeasurable commodity eternity becomes a common currency. It made more sense to talk about our reserved seats at Christ's banquet as it would to discuss any particulars of how he got caged. The man inside the man inside the box looked happier than he had any secular right to be. We joked about being sober but looking forward to whatever Jesus would be pouring at the feast. We talked about silverware at the King's table, would there be any, or would we eat falafel with our fingers? I told him a fanciful story about heaven being the place where, with spoons attached to our elbows, we fed each other, and hell being the place where we continually spilled everything just short of our mouths.

He asked to pray for my family to make up for the time I spent bawling at his mystical radiance.

I gave him the names of our sons and daughters, and grandchildren and got the name of his folks and brother. We put our hands up to the screen between us and I lost any sense of my hand being anything separate from the Spirit's. Our prayers had words, sounds, and groans, but it's real significance was that it happened. A bridge reflecting Christ's connection to us both was suddenly opened for traffic.

The marvel of a death row convicted criminal being Christ's first invited guest into heaven gave us an appreciation for hallowed ground being anyplace we stood together, gathered in His name. The risk of romanticizing the situation was tempered by the photo of the man's child taped above his bunk. It had been years since the boy smiled from a manicured lawn at someone with a camera, it would be years or something longer than years before the inmate would ever be able to ask his son if he remembered the day he spun and danced in his backyard. My son, a grown man sometimes clouded by drug addiction, was no closer to me physically than the inmates son was to him, so we closed every gap we could imagine in prayer. Our twenty minutes together ended with a promise of saving a seat for each other, and our boys, at His banquet table.

My partner was close to rapture with a former Mexican mafia hit man housed securely to protect him from death threats. The guard at that end of the walkway was nonplussed at the joy emanating from their connection. The watch change meant all conversation was to cease as quick as the drop of a grenade's pin on the floor in a war movie predicates an explosion. When that didn't happen a baton came out to keep time on the cage until our minister finally backed away from the singing inmate. Time waits for no one doing time, and the guard's impatience emphasized the gift of a few seconds peace is a very private thing, kept alive only in a compassionate heart.

We passed another half dozen unvisited cages. Maybe the men inside hadn't requested a visit, maybe they weren't believers, maybe they weren't even allowed the option. Pelican Bay holds over 1500 men in secure housing. We managed to meet three of them and felt the seed planted on each side of the gate was mustard sized and as significant as anything we did in three years of ministering to Pelican

Bay. The results, or consequences, of our willingness to visit the incarcerated are not always ours to know. Jesus said in Matthew 6:3 "But when you do a charitable deed, do not let your left hand know what your right hand is doing, that your charitable deed may be in secret; and your Father who sees in secret will Himself reward you openly."

The treasures we lay up in heaven may well be the saints we share a table with, I can hardly think of a crown that would shine as bright as the smile of being connected with loved ones at the celestial buffet. "All you can eat" signs may well be superseded by "All you can eat with, are welcome." Eating alone off a metal plate slid through a four inch slot is about as polar opposite of banqueting as we can devise. Bringing assurance that an afterlife gourmand existence may well be prepared for us in the face of our enemies is one thing, breaking the bread of our immediate attitudes and perceptions may well be a miracle approaching the scale of five fishes and two loaves.

What can be said? If the smallest stone in our shoe makes any thought of dancing intolerable, then perhaps sharing the knowledge of the Rock under our feet as the foundation of peace is music even the deafest of ears can fathom. Hebrews 11:1 says. "Faith is the substance of things hoped for, the evidence of things not seen." When the only view is three concrete walls and a wired cage, things 'not seen' can be a definite improvement. Keeping the faith is something we do in common. Fellowship with men in isolation is a way to pierce the impervious with the same nails that held Christ's arms open to the world.

The one missing sheep of every hundred could well be pacing a cell waiting for your voice and face to light up a rigorously contained world. To look like Jesus it is necessary to see like Jesus. Suffer the little children, that we all must become, to come into the Kingdom of God. His throne room is something we share face to face, eye to eye. It's true we have Jesus as a Friend in High Places, but it's in the lowest places that we need, and take, the most comfort.

Secure Housing Unit ministry may never be part of your prison experience. Even if it is, it is likely to be a sporadic addition to a more regular program. Research your facility's policy, be willing and trust the Spirit to move you through the screening procedures. If you make it to the cages it will be evident the Lord is ordering your steps. One foot in front of the other is the quickest path to our knees. Walking the walk is what the world, and the

Lord, wants of us. Walking the line is how we reach souls in the hole.

Chapter Nine

Family: The Ties that Unbind the Bound

A history of incarceration is common ground. I don't have a number or a graph but I would wager your family, like mine, has convicts, felons, or repeat offenders perched on various branches of the family tree. Depending on your economics, race, and neighborhood this may either shock you, or bore you with the flat bell tone of what else is new.

The regard an offender has for family can range from little more than resentment going in, to a treasured life line to the outside world. The most common prayer request we get from inmates is to pray for their families and the quickest most sincere response I experience is when I ask inmates to pray for mine.

I've no clue as to what God the Father went through seeing His Son in shackled custody. I do know seeing my son in an orange jump suit with handcuffs undid any composure I had about how life was supposed to be lived. A friend of mine measures anger by the likelihood of chewing concrete. My jaws tighten to the point of shattering molars when I'm angry. You can ask my dentist what fun it was to extract them because they were already splintered into shards.

I'll confess to mentally and emotionally, 'throwing away the key' a few times as my son's arrest resume` expanded. Rationalizing that being behind bars is the best place possible for a family member is a mental gymnastics maneuver stemming from a circus of unsavory characters, bold faced lies, and public consequences. How we get to the spectator side of the courtroom is hard to define as an answer to prayer, but there are many parents who hope their children are inside during the winter so they at least have a place to send a Christmas card.

Our enemy, Satan, doesn't have to worry about attacking the church, or sinking our nation, as long as our families are split by illegalities. The family that prays together sometimes starts that practice at sentencing. Jail and prison are very different things but the distinction is moot when visiting hours close. As prison ministers we step into a gap between family time and time served in a correctional facility.

The cliché` that we might be the only Jesus somebody ever meets is both magnified, and put under a microscope, when we seek to connect an inmate to the God of hope. Sharing eternity helps the time go faster. Coming back, again and again, works wonders. Our team travels an hour and a half to visit Pelican Bay State Prison once a month and the drive home is always rich with a sense of déjà vu` as if every visit is strung together into some extraordinary loop outside of real time.

We often remark that we are riding home on the hem of His garment. Touched and healed. We hope the men inside close the door to their inner rooms and seek the Lord knowing He is preparing mansions for us all. When Jesus raised the son of the widow of Nain (Luke 714-16) He touched the coffin and said, "Young man, I say to you arise." The watching crowds response to this resurrection exclaimed "God has visited His people." In a way we re-enact this miracle when we visit the inmates and encourage them to stand up in the love and mercy God has for us all.

The physical time spent with an incarcerated individual is as much part of the message of hope as anything we say or do. Eye contact precedes, and reveals, soul contact. When a visit is one on one it is sometimes defined by a wall of glass and a dangling phone line across a grey cubicle. Frustration is likely part of any thirty minute session. Phone codes to begin speaking might be forgotten or mis-dialed, the connections on out of date equipment distort voices, or fail, and conversations spill over from folks in the accompanying booths.

This is when reading faces can make our lives a living epistle. A set smile, a preconceived notion, a private agenda, make a mask and a mockery of our time facing a prisoner facing time. Simple, normalizing questions; "Did you sleep? Are you eating? Do you have anything to read?" help an inmate to relax and relate. The Peace that Jesus gives us is a balm to the soul searching, to the resentment, the blame, and doubt of a better future clouding an inmates mind. Our hands pressed to the glass represent the Hands pierced for our forgiveness.

So much is taken away from people serving a sentence. Whether it is 90 days in county, or life in a maximum security facility, contact with the outside world is a very personal restoration of dignity and self-worth. It is a thread of resuscitation back into intentional community. It is how our lives are woven together. It is the fabric of a shared faith. It is touching His garment.

The message of hope may spill over to the guards, the other jail employees, or other visitors in the waiting room. Casual talk is also causal. The cautionary rule; "Until a real Apostle shows up, you're it! "applies while waiting to go in as much as it does inside. Folks with folks inside might be gruff, they might be gregarious, but they all benefit from grace. I notice I get more polite than normal when I'm 'booted and suited' for jail ministry.

The sad thing is the full armor of God is not yet an automatic wardrobe. We must be conscious of body language, personal grooming, hygiene and attitudes as if every visit was in fact a reception to the banquet of Christ. The cliché` about being the only 'Jesus' some people will ever see carries over to the sense of smell. Baptisms need not be repeated but it is bad form to overpower the incense of our prayers with body odors or bad breath. If I weren't a convicted repeat offender of such a common courtesy I wouldn't mention it, the hope being this manual will help you avoid my mistakes as you make straight the way of the Lord.

First impressions have their merit, but the consistently repeated gesture of genuine brotherhood helps the imprisoned find their footing on the Rock. If we are unsure about knowing, or recognizing a prisoner, we make a point of asking if we've met before and if we haven't, a brief exchange of names and where we hail from can begin a new bridge to the calmer shore of the river of life. There is a certain joy, even a thrill in an inmate's voice when he reminds you of when you first met which springs from a happiness in the simple act of returning.

The first time inside is likely to be such a wave of emotion that you come out drenched but don't remember getting your feet wet. The second visit is almost as much to confirm what you remember from the first time as it is to chart any future involvement and by the third time through the gate, the reality of the opportunity to make a difference begins to take shape.

This where we share the Gospel without using words. In a way we are behind enemy lines, but we behave as guests to infiltrate the hearts of those around us. What is said and shared colors the impression of the visit but the time shared is the event. One doesn't go for a massage because of the ambient flute music. Aching muscles need kneading. The heart is also a muscle. It needs needing.

In Matthew 11:28 Jesus tells us to come to Him to learn to be gentle and humble in heart. He promises we will find rest for our souls Entering into God's rest is not a call to inactivity. It is in rest that we can come boldly to the throne of grace to obtain mercy in times of need (Hebrews 4:16) What we obtain, and bring to a visit, we can share. Peace of mind, rest for the soul, gentleness for the heart. "Today, if you will hear His voice, do not harden your hearts." What He whispers, we are to shout from the rooftops, from the highest places we can imagine. Sitting across from an inmate in a plastic chair could very well be such a place.

Short timers might want to talk about what happens when they get out, lifers tend to focus on families and the folks back home. The most serious request for counsel I ever received came from a Buddhist trustee who sat in the adjacent library during our services. He approached as I was packing up my saxophone and said, "Excuse me Pastor, but how do you be a good person when you are surrounded by bad ones?"

Ever the prepared theologian I asked why he thought I knew the answer any better than he did. He sat down on the floor and smiled in one of those 'when the student is willing the teacher appears' positions that are the probable cause of my knee trouble. I told him when Jesus was asked a similar question by a rich young man He responded by saying ,"No one is good but One, that is, God." (Matthew 19:17) indicating being good is the wrong target. Being considerate, being compassionate, uncovering what is common about common sense is the playing field, and if he felt he could do it on his own he should do it on his own, if he didn't, he might try praying to the One whom Jesus called good for wisdom, grace, and mercy.

A few months later the man was passing out foot long submarine sandwiches at our Easter banquet and he gave me a smile and a nod. When it came time to get my plate, which was also weighed down with four slices of pizza, he leaned over to tell me, "It works." Ever cognizant of the subtle realities of intimate conversation I asked him, "What works?"

"Prayer to the One who is good. I'm less nervous about offending people, or being offended. It works Pastor. You were right!"

I wanted to beam in some radiant, but appropriately humble, pride at having been useful to the man's spiritual journey, but mostly I was grateful the young man was useful in mine.

Jesus marveled when He found faith in the Roman centurion. He told him, "Go your way; and as you believed, so let it be done for you." I believe He is still saying the same thing to you and I, and the many that will come from the east and the west, and sit down with Abraham, Isaac, and Jacob in the kingdom of heaven.

What we believe about God and what we, and the inmates, believe about ourselves is the mission field, the battlefield. Jesus was killed for asking us to believe Him. Christians are still killed today for believing in Him, but the greater crime might be us killing our faith by not putting it into action. Visiting the incarcerated is the least we can do for the least of these. You may find a key to heaven by unlocking the mystery of prison ministry.

San Quentin

Thieves come against locks
on windows, locks on doors.
Your heart can't be stolen
when you give it away.

If your hand be extended,
an inmate befriended,
the crime of isolation
caves in.

At the bars or behind 'em,
lonely is where you find 'em,
the trouble on their faces
is a sin.

We pretend we can't be busted,
convince ourselves we're trusted, but
it's only by His Grace
they let us in.

His Light is not to blind them,

your smile never random,

start by trading places

from within.

Chapter Ten

Where to go from Here

Folks go to jail for crimes they did, or didn't, commit. Ministers go to jail for different reasons. The standard issues include spreading the Gospel, saving souls, giving hope, comfort, and counsel. Personal reasons might include family history with incarceration, trying to build up a preaching resume`, or an undeniable sense of being useful, like a foot in the door of despair, keeping it from clanging shut.

To get started, review the policies of facilities near you, say within one hundred miles. Begin the paperwork. If you are affiliated with a church get council from your Pastor. If someone already heads up a prison ministry join the team, if not try on the hat, one size fits all.

My hope in writing this book of encouraging anecdotes is that new people will take up the challenge. I look forward to meeting you at the gate, the pearly one, with Jesus Inside. Amen.

Will Schmit is a volunteer minister of the Gospel at Pelican Bay State Prison in California. He is a contributing blogger to www.InspireAFire.com and offers original praise poetry at Christian Tourist Syndrome Podcast as well as www.christiantouristsyndrome.blogspot.com.

www.ingramcontent.com/pod-product-compliance
Lightning Source LLC
Chambersburg PA
CBHW050119280326
41933CB00010B/1171